# Cyprus

# TOP 10 ATTRACTIONS

**The church at Lagoudera** • One of the island's celebrated frescoed churches *(page 62)*

**Cyprus Museum** • A must-see in Nicosia, housing the island's finest collection of antiquities *(page 33)*

**Keryneia** • Its harbour is Cyprus' most picturesque *(page 79)*

**Stavrovouni Monastery** • This historic landmark has magnificent views from its hill-top position *(page 45)*

**Agia Napa** • Beaches of golden sand have made it the island's top destination for sun seekers (page 46)

**Famagusta** • The old town holds a number of architectural curiosities, including Venetian fortifications (page 81)

**Aphrodite's Birthplace** • According to legend, Petra tou Romiou is the very spot where the goddess came ashore (page 57)

**Akamas Peninsula** • The last great coastal wilderness of southern Cyprus, is best explored off road (page 74)

**Agios Neofytos Monastery** • The focus here is the hermit's chapel and cell (page 72)

**Kourion** • The ancient clifftop site is one of the island's archaeological highlights (page 53)

# CONTENTS

95

39

26

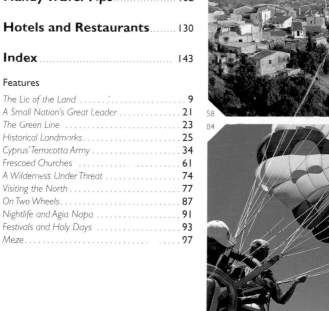

92

58

84

# INTRODUCTION

Cyprus made its ancient fortune from copper, a chunk of history that's echoed today in one of the colours that make up the Republic's national flag. In modern times, Cyprus' greatest natural resource is sunshine, around 340 days every year. Yet 'Aphrodite's Island' has sometimes been careless with the coastline that takes advantage of all that sun shine. Many resorts are large and over-developed, with little of immediately obvious historical or cultural character, and the battle to preserve the remaining unspoiled coastline is being closely fought. But you don't have to delve far to begin to appreciate this island. A little way inland are countless old villages, a constellation of vineyards, and rugged mountain ranges that are great places of escape. The layers of a long and tangled history, from Stone Age peoples, through Greeks, Persians, Romans, Byzantines, Crusaders, Turks and British, are there to be seen and felt.

An idyllic beach scene

Some of your finest memories are likely to be of a remarkably friendly and hospitable people – both Greek-Cypriot and Turkish-Cypriot. Considering their turbulent and traumatic recent history, you have to marvel at the Cypriots' easy-going nature. This is, after all, an island that was invaded by Turkey and split in two in 1974. At a stroke, some 170,000 Greek Cypriots

The remains of a Graeco-Roman temple at Kourion

The grape harvest

became refugees in their own country, and were forced to flee to the south of the island. At the same time, around 30,000 Turkish Cypriots moved north. The island is still divided today, though since 2003 there has been greater freedom of movement across the border.

Although it's now much easier to visit the North (which only Turkey recognises as a separate republic), most travellers still choose the Greek-Cypriot South. But for those who do go across the line that separates the two parts of the island, the North offers a much less commercialised landscape, including some pristine beaches and many more varieties of flora and fauna.

## An Easy-Going People

Through all the turmoil, the Greek Cypriots have managed to retain a sunny disposition. The Greeks are by nature a friendly, hospitable people, but Cypriots seem to take this a stage further. Ask a couple harvesting grapes if you can take their photo, and they will not only strike a happy pose, but also gather a large bag of grapes for you to take home. Compliment a chef on the quality of his *sheftalia* at a taverna and chat to him about village life, and he may well insist that lunch is on the house. Chat to an old man about Makarios and the EOKA days, and you'll notice 15 minutes later that he has left his family waiting in order to talk to a complete stranger. It is rare that a visitor leaves Cyprus without some tale of the people's generosity.

It is not a mere marketing gimmick that often at the end of a meal, coffee and a liqueur (even if it is the throat-charring *zivania*) is provided on the house. As you will probably hear said more than once, 'It is our custom'. You don't have to go to the most remote mountain village for such hospitality, but it is also true that you are much less likely to find this warmth in the more obviously tourist-oriented watering holes.

This widespread cheerfulness is coupled with a dignity that shuns expansive Latin gestures. The British like to think that their presence on the island over the past century has been at least partly responsible and, as far as the politeness of the

## The Lie of the Land

Tucked into the northeast corner of the Mediterranean between Turkish Anatolia and Syria, Cyprus is the Mediterranean's third largest island, after Sicily and Sardinia. Its land surface of 9,251 sq km (3,572 sq miles) sandwiches the broad Mesaoria Plain between two chains of mountains – the Pentadaktylos range in the northeast and the Troodos in the southwest. Three major rivers, which run dry in summer, originate in the Troodos Mountains: the Pediaios flowing east to Famagusta Bay, the Karyoti west to Morfou Bay, and the Kouris south to Episkopi. The highest peak is Mt Olympos, at 1,951m (6,401ft).

**Population:** Around 900,000 in the South; 265,000 in the North, including 80,000 post-1974 Turkish settlers.

**Capital:** Nicosia (Lefkosia/Lefkosa): 220,000 in the Greek-Cypriot city; 41,000 in the Turkish-Cypriot sector.

**Major Cities:** South: Limassol (Lemesos; 173,000), Larnaka (77,000), Pafos (52,000). North: Famagusta (Ammochostos/Gazimağusa; 36,000), Morfou (Güzelyurt; 13,000), Keryneia (Girne; 14,000).

police and the sober honesty of public officials are concerned, they may be right. But the courtesy of Cypriots in general seems to be a more deeply ingrained quality.

## Troubled Relations

A more sombre note is struck when the matter of the divided island is raised. Greek-Cypriot refugees from the North react more with melancholy than anger. Nostalgically, restaurants and shops in Larnaka or Limassol may bear the names of their lost homes in Famagusta, Keryneia or Belapais.

Sadly, because of its geographical position, Cyprus has always been continually beset by unwelcome visitors. Apart from attracting Phoenician and Assyrian pirates, and conquerors from Egypt, Persia, Greece and Turkey, Cyprus has been the easy prey of French crusaders and Venetian and Genoese merchants. It was even a pawn in the last days of the

**Pano Lefkara in the Troodos Mountains**

British Empire. In his book *Bitter Lemons*, Lawrence Durrell, who spent time in Cyprus as a teacher and colonial official, revealed just how paternalistic even the best-intentioned British observer could be in the 1950s.

## The Island's Attractions

But for today's visitors, the traces of the past are a compelling reason for coming. There are the ancient Greek and Roman ruins at Kourion and Salamis, the splendid Roman mosaics at Pafos, the crusader castles of Kolossi and the Pentadakylos Mountains, and the Byzantine monasteries and churches of the Troodos Mountains.

Cyprus is also a country of unsung natural beauty. While the resort beaches cater for holidaymakers happy to lie baking in serried ranks, the coastline, particularly of the Akamas Peninsula, has enough rugged cliffs and surf-beaten coves to appeal to the romantic individualist or rugged off-road biker. Inland, the Troodos Mountains are a wild and spectacularly verdant adventure of hairpin curves and restored forest. Sprinkled like forgotten gems in the landscape are tiny Byzantine churches, secrets known only to their parishioners for centuries. Today, 10 of these are on the UNESCO protected list and no visit to Cyprus is complete without visiting at least one of them.

Meanwhile, in the plains of the interior, villages untouched by tourism nestle among olive groves and citrus orchards, and goats and sheep scamper among forgotten ancient ruins. Vineyards climb the sunny hillsides, cypress trees frame a somnolent abbey or the skeleton of an abandoned fortress, and rural Cypriot life continues at a gentle pace.

## Distinctive features

In some ways Cyprus is quite British, although in other ways it seems very exotic. Nothing illustrates this contrast better than the juxtaposition of a mosque (seen in most big towns) with the cosiest of British relics, the traditional pillar box.

# A BRIEF HISTORY

The first records of human presence in Cyprus seem to be those of a group who were nomads and hunters rather than permanently settled. Tools and butchered animal bones found in a cave at Akrotiri on the south coast are dated at about 9000BC; the bones are thought to be those of indigenous pygmy hippopotamuses and pygmy elephants killed on the beach by seafarers who landed briefly on the island. The earliest traces of permanent settlers are stone beehive-shaped dwellings at the tip of the Karpasia Peninsula and at the inland site of Choirokoitia, which date back to at least 5800BC.

By 3500BC, copper was being mined in the Troodos foothills and Cyprus began to prosper as a trading centre, with goods coming in from Asia, Egypt, Crete, the Peloponnese and the Aegean Islands in exchange for Cypriot pottery, copperware and opium. After 1600BC, large numbers of fortresses were built around the island, which suggests a period of conflict. Copper was sent to mighty Egypt as protection money and, in exchange, the Pharaoh called the king of Cyprus 'brother'.

## Greeks, Persians and Romans

Upheaval in the Peloponnese, caused variously by natural calamities and invasions from the north, drove Mycenaean Greeks east across the Mediterranean, and some settled in Cyprus. From 1200BC, they established city-kingdoms at Enkomi (Egkomi), replaced later by Salamis (near modern Famagusta), Kition (now Larnaka), Kourion, Palaia Pafos (Kouklia), Soloi, Lapithos and other places. The island acquired the predominantly Greek identity it was never entirely to relinquish. Temples were erected near smelting workshops, presided over by Aphrodite, the goddess of love and fertility.

As the Persian Empire spread across the eastern Mediterranean in the 6th century BC, Cyprus, along with other Greek islands, was annexed. In 499BC it joined the Ionian Greek revolt but, after heroic resistance, notably during the long siege of Palaia Pafos, was crushed by the Persians the next year.

In 333BC, Alexander the Great ended Persian dominance in the eastern Mediterranean and placed Cyprus under Macedonian rule. After his death in 323BC, the island was a battleground as his generals fought over the succession, flattening many ancient cities in the process. By 299BC, Ptolemy I emerged the victor, the city-kingdoms disappeared and Cyprus became part of the Hellenistic state of Egypt. The Ptolemies ruled for 250 years until the Romans, on a pretext that the island was harbouring pirates, annexed it in 58BC to their province of Cilicia (southern Turkey).

Replica mosaic of *Leda and the Swan* at Kouklia (see page 71)

In 47BC, Julius Caesar made a present of Cyprus to Cleopatra, the last ruler of the Ptolemaic dynasty. After her suicide, Augustus took it back for the Romans and let King Herod of Judaea farm out the Cypriot copper mines to Jewish entrepreneurs.

## The Byzantine Era

Despite the apostle Paul's mission to Cyprus in AD45, the Hellenistic islanders continued in their attachment to

Detail of a terracotta figurine dating from the 5th century BC

the cults of Aphrodite and, with the growth of highly prized vineyards, the wine god Dionysos. Only in the 4th century, as Christianity took a hold on the Roman leadership, did churches and monasteries begin to spring up across Cyprus. In AD330, the mother of the Roman emperor Constantine, Helena, is said to have visited the island and founded the great Stavrovouni Monastery.

Priests wielded considerable power over everyday life, defending peasants against tax collectors, but also demanding unquestioning allegiance. In 488, the archbishop of Cyprus gained total control over the island's spiritual affairs and began to carry a royal sceptre rather than a pastoral staff, wore a cloak of imperial purple and signed his name in imperial red ink – rights that the archbishops retain to this day.

With the Byzantine Empire weak from its war against Persia, the Arabs took the opportunity to cross over to Cyprus in 649 with a fleet of 1,500 ships. Salamis (now Constantia) was left in such ruins that it never recovered; the raid continued across the island until news of an approaching Byzantine fleet prompted retreat.

Four years later, in a move that foreshadowed events of the 20th century, the Arabs staged a second invasion and left a garrison of 12,000 men, encouraging Muslim immigration to establish a foothold on the island. The Byzantines and the Muslim Caliphate subsequently agreed to neutralise Cyprus – there would be no military bases, though ports could be used for refitting the navy – and also to share tax revenues. Over the next 300 years, Muslims and Christians engaged in offshore battles and launched raids against each other, but also lived side by side.

## The Crusades

During the time of the Crusades, Cyprus became a key strategic post for Byzantine interests in Syria and Palestine. The governor organised protection for pilgrims to the Holy Land and supervised the rebuilding of Jerusalem's Church of the Holy Sepulchre and fortifications for its Christian Quarter. The invasion of Ottoman Turks in Anatolia and the Levant after 1071 threatened communications with Constantinople, but Cyprus was still able to supply food to soldiers in the First Crusade of 1097 and even provided refuge for defeated Muslim princes.

A Stavrovouni mosaic depicts Byzantine-era Christianity

New trade developed with Venice and the young Crusader states on the mainland. However, the Turks' conquest of Anatolia in 1176 isolated Cyprus from the Byzantine government. Isaac Comnenos, a junior member of the imperial family, felt free to make himself the despotic 'Emperor' of Cyprus, using Sicilian mercenaries to fight off the Byzantine fleet.

Salvation from his brutal rule came in the form of England's King Richard the Li-

**Asset stripper**

Although King Richard deposed the 'emperor' Comnenos, he stripped the island of all its money to pay for his expedition to the Holy Land, and Greeks were denied any governing role. They were even ordered to shave off their beards, the supreme humiliation.

onheart, who docked at Limassol on his way to the Crusades. He crushed Comnenos and was welcomed by cheering crowds in Nicosia. After a few months, Richard left the island in the hands of Guy de Lusignan, a French former king of Jerusalem. Lusignan introduced barons from war torn Palestine with the promise of a safer life on Cyprus' fertile (and free) farm estates. The Lusignan dynasty's feudal rule reduced native Cypriots to serfdom. In 1260, the Roman Catholic Church was declared supreme on the island, though Orthodox priests maintained their status as the real spiritual authority inside the Greek-Cypriot community.

## Genoese and Venetians

During the 14th century, Cyprus profited greatly as a Christian outpost, supplying the crusaders. Famagusta's merchants in particular became renowned for their extravagant wealth. The island's opulence attracted pirates, and fuelled a heated rivalry between the merchants of Genoa and Venice that erupted in bloody riots in 1345. The Cypriots sided with the Venetians against the Genoese, murdering merchants and looting shops in Famagusta. In retaliation, Genoa sent a fleet to ravage the whole island. In 1374, they extorted reparations of two million gold florins and confiscated the port of Famagusta.

By now, the Lusignan kings had become too weak to resist Italian demands. James II needed help from the Sultan of Egypt to oust the Genoese in 1464, but the gold it cost him emptied his treasury. By various intrigues, the Venetians stepped into the breach and ruled Cyprus for the next 82 years.

The Venetians' lucrative trade was threatened by Ottoman encroachment on three sides – Anatolia, the Levant and Egypt. In 1570, the Turks demanded that Venice give up Cyprus. Imagining that attack would come from the east, the Venetians consolidated their defences mainly in Famagusta. But the Turks landed on the south coast and took Nicosia in 46 days. The capital's Venetian commander was killed and his head sent as a warning to Marcantonio Bragadino, the commander at Famagusta. Undeterred, Bragadino led a heroic defence of the port city, with 8,000 Greek-Cypriot and Italian troops holding out for over 10 months against a Turkish army that was said to number 200,000. On 1 August 1571, with his ammunition gone, Bragadino surrendered. He was promised safe passage, but when the Turks saw they had lost 50,000 men to such a tiny army, they flayed Bragadino alive. Cyprus was now a province of the Ottoman Empire.

To defend their trade, the Venetians fortified Famagusta

Pafos Fort, used by the Turkish and the British

## Turkish Rule

With the Turks controlling the whole of the eastern Mediterranean, Cyprus lost its strategic importance and was left to stagnate. The administrators proved more idle than oppressive and the island's infrastructure fell into ruin. The only advantage for the Greek Cypriots was the regained status of the Orthodox Church. By 1660, the Sultan made their archbishop directly responsible for the Cypriot citizenry.

During the Greek War of Independence of 1821, Archbishop Kyprianos let Greek rebel ships pick up supplies on the north coast. Turkey immediately sent in 4,000 Syrian troops. The archbishop and three of his bishops were executed. More troops were brought in from Egypt, resulting in large-scale massacres and the plunder of church property.

Over the next 50 years, the Sultan tried to halt widespread abuses by Turkish tax collectors, which were provoking massive emigration of both Greek and Turkish Cypriots. But local Turkish officials opposed all reforms, often resorting to armed intimidation of governors sent in by the Sultan. The disintegration of Ottoman authority in Cyprus was symptomatic of the imminent collapse of the empire.

## The British Step In

With 'the sick man of Europe' on his deathbed, the superpowers of the time hovered around like vultures to pick at the remains, among which Cyprus was a choice morsel. Britain was concerned that the eastern Mediterranean should remain safe for its ships to pass through the Suez Canal to India. To keep Russia out, Britain signed the Cyprus Convention with Turkey, whereby the island came under British administration while formally remaining the Sultan's possession. In 1878, the deal was sealed with a peaceful ceremony in Nicosia.

Greek Cypriots were happy about the transfer of power from corrupt Turks to upright Britons, and came to appreciate the new schools, hospitals, law courts and roads that had become the hallmarks of British colonial administration. The population rose from 186,000 in 1881 to 310,000 in 1921. But the most important contribution they expected from the British would be to help Cyprus achieve *enosis*, or union with Greece, as Britain had done for the Ionian Islands in 1864. As long as he was in opposition, Gladstone supported the claim, but he did nothing about it when he became prime minister.

Union with Greece was, of course, opposed by the Turkish-Cypriots. They usually remained calm, confident that Britain would respect its alliance with Turkey and not give in to demands for *enosis*.

In 1914, Turkey sided with Germany in World War I and Britain promptly annexed Cyprus, claiming it as a British Crown Colony. More roads were built, but little was done to-

Statue of Archbishop
Makarios in Nicosia

wards *enosis*. In 1931, impatient Greek-Cypriot members of the Legislative Council resigned, and riots broke out in Nicosia. Troops were brought in from Egypt. Insurgent bishops were deported, political parties banned, the Greek flag outlawed and press censorship imposed. But during World War II, in response to the British alliance with Greece against Germany, Cypriots rallied to the British flag and furnished 30,000 troops. Political parties were duly reinstated.

## The Fight for Unity

In 1945, Britain thought it was doing Cyprus a favour by moving it towards self-rule. But the slogan of the day was '*enosis* and only *enosis*'. In 1950 a plebiscite of Greek Cypriots voted 96 percent in favour of union with Greece, and the Church appointed a new leader, Archbishop Makarios III *(see right)*.

In 1955, the campaign for *enosis* became an armed struggle, led by Lieutenant-Colonel George Grivas, a Cypriot-born Greek Army officer. Directed from a hideout deep in the Troodos Mountains, EOKA (the Greek initials for the National Organisation of Cypriot Fighters) conducted a campaign of bombing public buildings and assassinating opponents of *enosis*. Archbishop Makarios publicly disowned the actions, but gave EOKA clandestine support. He was exiled in 1956, first to the Seychelles and then to Athens.

In Greece itself the public gave noisy support to the Greek-Cypriot cause, but their government was reticent.

Turkey supported the Turkish-Cypriot opposition to *enosis* with two main arguments: the Muslim community would be defenceless if it was swallowed up in the greater Greek nation; and Greek extension to Cyprus would pose a military threat to Turkey. In 1958, Turkish Cypriots rioted in favour of partitioning the island.

In 1959, the Turkish and Greek Cypriots met in Zurich, agreeing to renounce both *enosis* and partition, while guaranteeing strict safeguards to protect the Turkish-Cypriot minority. The president of the new independent republic would be Greek-Cypriot Archbishop Makarios, and his vice-president would be the Turkish-Cypriot leader, Fazil Küçük. On 16 August 1960, Cyprus became independent, though still part of the British Commonwealth (with Britain retaining two military bases on the south coast). Grivas retired, unhappy, to Athens.

## A Small Nation's Great Leader

In Archbishop Makarios, Cyprus was blessed with a first president of great intellect and spiritual authority. Born in 1913 to a peasant family in the Troodos Mountains, Mihail Christodoulous Mouskos became a monk at Kykkos Monastery. He studied in Athens and then Boston, before returning to Cyprus in 1948 to become Bishop of Kition (Larnaka).

Archbishop at the young age of 37, he won popular support with his dignified eloquence. But he was criticised by foreign observers for his failure to control Greek-Cypriot extremists, thus provoking alarm among Turkish Cypriots. Makarios, who died in 1977, impressed the world with his moral leadership of non-aligned nations at the height of the Cold War, and his courage during the Greek-inspired coup against him in 1974 and the subsequent Turkish invasion.

Kykkos Monastery, reputedly an EOKA base in the 1950s

## Troubled Independence

Cabinet posts, parliamentary seats and civil service jobs were apportioned to Greek and Turkish Cypriots according to a fair ratio, and the main towns elected separate Greek- and Turkish-Cypriot municipal governments, but the constitution proved too complex to work. In 1963, Makarios proposed 13 simplifying amendments which the Turkish Cypriots vetoed, and fighting broke out in Nicosia. The British supervised a cease-fire and set up a 'Green Line' *(see right)* separating the communities. United Nations forces were brought in to patrol the Green Line in March 1964, and they have stayed ever since. Turkish-Cypriot enclaves were formed mainly in the northern part of the island, and Turkey and Greece each sent in officers to train local forces.

In 1974, in a bid to gain popularity at home, Greece's military junta tried to impose *enosis* on Cyprus. Makarios resisted, demanding that the Greek officers withdraw. The junta responded by engineering a military attack on the Presidential Palace in Nicosia. Makarios escaped to Pafos and broadcast to the people of Cyprus, refuting reports of his assassination. This coup d'état gave Turkey a pretext to invade. Within three weeks, Turkish troops had occupied most of northern Cyprus. Makarios escaped to New York, where he rallied support in the UN to reinstate him as president. He died in 1977. The Turkish army remained in control of 37 percent of the island, including Famagusta, northern Nicosia and Keryneia. Some 170,000 Greek Cypriots were forced to flee to the south, while about 30,000 Turkish Cypriots migrated to the north. By 2005, approximately 80,000 settlers had been brought into Northern Cyprus from Turkey.

In 1983, the so-called Turkish Republic of Northern Cyprus was set up with Rauf Denktash as President, but it was recognised only by Turkey. The UN condemned the move and urged the leaders to find a way other than partition to protect minority rights on the island. Due to the diplomatic isolation of the Turkish north, the economy in the region stagnated. Greek Cypriots, on the other hand, recovered well from the shock of invasion; their economy thrived thanks mainly, but not exclusively, to tourism.

In 1998 the government of southern Cyprus entered into negotiations about possible entry into the European Union. The EU expressed a preference for Cyprus to join as a unit-

## The Green Line

The Green Line, which marks the division between north and south Cyprus, owes its name to the British army officer who drew a line in green ink on a map which approximated the de facto border. This became the official buffer zone. The Turkish name for the border is the Attila Line, after the code name Operation Attila for the 1974 invasion. The line, which had been open for transit by non-Cypriot visitors from the South to the North under strictly controlled conditions, was opened in 2003 to freer movement in both directions, including by Cypriots. Since then the number of crossing points has increased and the terms of transit have been further relaxed.

ed country – a move that prompted various efforts towards peace and reunification. In April 2003 there was a shift in the stalemate over cross-border movement. In that month Denktash opened the Green Line *(see page 23)* and allowed citizens of both sides almost unconditional access.

Turkish-Cypriot elections in December 2003 paved the way for a further relaxing of the relationship. But additional UN talks held in early 2004 faltered just weeks ahead of the date set for the accession of Cyprus – at least the Greek-Cypriot South – to the EU. The UN's proposed agreement was put to referenda in both parts of the island. The Turkish Cypriots voted in favour and the Greek Cypriots against.

In 2004, the Republic of Cyprus joined the EU without Northern Cyprus. But momentum towards a settlement seemed to be growing. A new round of UN-sponsored consultations began in 2005, leading to a meeting between the leaders of the two sides the following year.

In March 2007, the Greek Cypriots unilaterally demolished their barricades at the Green Line on Odos Lidras (Ledra Street), which was Nicosia's main commercial artery before the capital was divided. The Turkish Cypriots promptly did the same on their side. Military and political agreements, plus de-mining and securing derelict buildings, are required before a new crossing point can be opened up. Pending these, the action remains a symbolic gesture, but it is potentially an important one.

**Tourism has enabled the Greek-Cypriot economy to thrive**

## Historical Landmarks

**c. 9000BC** First evidence of human occupation.

**c. 7000BC** First permanent settlements on Cyprus.

**c. 3500BC** Copper mines in Troodos foothills establish early wealth.

**1200BC** Mycenaean Greeks settle on the island.

**700–350BC** Invasions by Assyrians and Persians.

**333BC** Alexander the Great establishes Macedonian rule.

**299BC** Cyprus joins Hellenistic Egypt under the Ptolemy dynasty.

**58BC** Romans annexe Cyprus to their empire.

**4th century AD** Christianity takes hold; many churches built.

**653** Arabs invade and install a garrison on the island.

**965–1185** Middle Byzantine period. Cyprus flourishes.

**1191–2** England's Richard the Lionheart defeats Isaac Comnenos and transfers the island to Guy de Lusignan, who founds a 300-year dynasty.

**14th–15th centuries** Cyprus grows rich from supplying crusaders but is pillaged by Genoese. Venetians take over from the Lusignans.

**1571** Fall of Famagusta to the Turks ends Venetian rule.

**1571–1878** Period of Turkish rule.

**1878–1914** Cyprus under British administration, with Turkish possession. Turkey sides with Germany in 1914, so Britain annexes Cyprus.

**1931** *Enosis* (unity with Greece) campaign builds force with riots.

**1955** EOKA begins campaign of violence in pursuit of *enosis*.

**1959–64** Turkish and Greek Cypriots form joint administration that leads to independence in 1960, but breaks down. UN intervenes.

**1974** Coup by Greek military junta gives Turkey pretext to invade, occupying 37 percent of island.

**1983** The 'Turkish Republic of Northern Cyprus' is declared by the North, but recognised only by Turkey.

**2003** The Green Line in Nicosia is opened to relatively free movement between both sectors of the city.

**2004** The Republic of Cyprus joins the EU without Northern Cyprus.

**2007** The Greek Cypriots demolish military barricades in Nicosia.

**2008** The euro is introduced in the South on 1 January.

# WHERE TO GO

If you really want to get to know Cyprus, rather than just soak up the sun on its beaches, you should plan to stay in more than one place. If your base is at one of South Cyprus' extremities – Pafos or Agia Napa – it's a good idea to spend a night or two at a more central coastal location, such as Limassol or Larnaka, or to go inland to Nicosia or the Troodos Mountains. With the North much more accessible than before, you may want to set aside time for this region.

> **Buffer zone**
>
> Never refer to the Green Line as 'the border' in front of a Greek Cypriot, as this implies that you recognise it officially as such. Call it 'the buffer zone'.

## NICOSIA AND ENVIRONS

Amid the animated prosperity of the Nicosia's southern sector, it is easy to forget the stretches of wall and barbed wire that make the still-divided capital look like a reluctant successor to Berlin. But with movement across the Green Line far simpler and freer now, the barrier has lost at least some of its sting.

Nicosia (*Lefkosia* in Greek, *Lefkoşa* in Turkish) is Cyprus' only inland city. For tourists, almost everything of interest is confined within, or just outside, the old city walls. Many visitors just spend a day here, but if you also want to allot a full day for exploring Turkish-Cypriot north Nicosia (for Northern Cyprus, *see pages 75–83)*, it's best to stay overnight. Be prepared for real heat. Nicosia is always around five degrees hotter than on the coast, with temperatures soaring well over 30°C (86°F) in July and August.

**Clear waters at Aphrodite's Birthplace on the southwest coast**

Situated on the site of ancient Ledra, today's city was founded in the 3rd century BC by Lefkos, son of Ptolemy I of Egypt. When the coastal towns of Pafos and Salamis came under Arab attack in the 7th century AD, the population shifted to the interior and Nicosia became the chief city. Under the Lusignans, it evolved into a splendid capital marked by elegant churches and monasteries in the French Gothic style.

Just prior to the Turkish invasion of 1570, the Venetians built the city's massive defensive wall. The city held out for just seven weeks before the Ottoman Turks broke in and slaughtered 20,000 of its citizens. In a modern-day echo of those brutal times, some of the heaviest fighting of the 1974 Turkish invasion took place around here. The eerie buffer zone, with its burnt-out, deserted buildings, UN checkpoints, barbed wire, sandbags and roadblocks, has become the city's most unwelcome tourist attraction. However, just a few metres away, you'll find a composed and buoyant city.

## The Fortifications

The ramparts hurriedly built by the Venetians remain Nicosia's dominant feature. Indeed, with its 11 pointed bastions and three giant gateways, the wheel-shaped Renaissance fortification has become the modern capital's distinctive logo.

**Sturdy Famagusta Gate**

The gates bear the names of the three coastal cities to which they lead. The Keryneia Gate is in Turkish-controlled northern Nicosia, where it is called the Girne Gate. The massive tunnel-like **Famagusta Gate**, to the east, was originally the main entrance to the old city. It has been restored and is used as a cultural centre. The stone barrel vaults provide an excellent setting for concerts, plays and modern art exhibitions, but it is only open to the public when an event is scheduled. By contrast, the **Pafos Gate**, to the west, is a small, unglamorous affair, surrounded by UN installations and the vestiges of war. Some of the bastions shelter municipal offices, while sections of the (now dry) moat serve as public gardens, playgrounds and car parks.

Omeriye Mosque

## The Old City

Today, most visitors to the old city enter through **Plateia Eleftherias**, a prominent square and home to the Town Hall. Off the square runs the old city's principal thoroughfare, **Odos Lidras**. This pedestrian street is usually thronged with shoppers. Near the southern end, at 17 Odos Ippokratous, is the award-winning **Leventis Municipal Museum of Nicosia** (open Tue–Sun 10am–4.30pm; free but a donation appreciated), which presents a beautifully designed account of Nicosia's history. Displayed in a fine 19th-century neoclassical mansion, the exhibits include costumes, utensils, coins and ceramics.

Just behind the museum is the revived **Laïki Geitonia** (Popular Neighbourhood), which purports to recreate the

### Walking tours

There is an office of the Cyprus Tourism Organisation in the Laïki Geitonia (at 11 Odos Aristokyprou), from which free walking tours of the city depart on Monday, Thursday, and Friday at 10am.

atmosphere of old Nicosia. Although it is actually a slightly contrived tourist enclave, it's a very popular spot that is particularly pretty at night. Various buildings in traditional style, some restored, others specially constructed, house quaint shops and tavernas, plus artisans' galleries where you can watch the craftsmen at work.

The municipal tourist information office here is worth a visit if only to watch the 15-minute video on the history of the city. For even better views of 'the other side', go to the museum-observatory on the top floor of the Shakolas department store on Odos Lidras.

Northeast of Laïki Geitonia, walk along Odos Aischylou and turn right on Odos Liasidou towards the minaret landmark of **Omeriye Mosque**, which was transformed from the Augustinian monastery church of St Mary's by the city's 16th-century Turkish conquerors. It is still used as a mosque by Muslim worshippers living in or visiting the Greek-Cypriot sector, and is open to visitors (don't forget to remove your shoes).

Now head northwest to the landmark **Faneromeni Church**. Although it only dates from 1872–3 in its present form, it is a mix of several styles and features a fine iconostasis. Alongside it is a small, squat, ancient mosque, which is usually closed to the public. From here continue along Odos Nikokleous to return to Odos Lidras.

Odos Lidras terminates at the **buffer zone**, where on a raised viewing point, manned by Greek-Cypriot soldiers, you can peer into the desolate no-man's land between South and North Cyprus.

## The Archbishop's Palace

On the eastern side of the city, on Plateia Archiepiskopou Kyprianou, the **Archbishop's Palace** is a curious modern pastiche of Venetian architecture. Amid the splendour of the state rooms (occasionally open for tours), Archbishop Makarios III installed an austere bedroom with a simple iron bed.

Housed in the public wing of the palace is one of the island's finest museums, the **Byzantine Museum and Art Galleries**  (open Mon–Fri 9am–4.30pm, Sat 9am–1pm; admission fee). This institution has rescued and restored a superb collection of icons from all over Cyprus. Presented with loving care, it offers the island's full range of Byzantine art, from a primitive 9th-century Virgin Mary to some examples that demonstrate the genre's decline in the 18th century. Don't miss the display of 33 splendid mosaics from Panagia Kanakaria church in Northern Cyprus, which were recovered through court action in the 1990s, after having been looted and offered for sale on the international art market.

An icon of Christ on display at the Byzantine Museum

Next to the museum is **Agios Ioannis** (St John's; open Mon–Fri 8am–noon and 2–4pm, Sat 8am–noon; free), Nicosia's small Orthodox cathedral, built in 1665 in an approximation of Late Gothic style. Its colourful

18th-century frescoes, which cover the walls and ceiling, depict landmarks in the island's early Christian history.

The adjacent Gothic-arcaded monastery building, which was the Archbishop's Palace before the present one was built, is now the **Ethnographic Museum of Cyprus** (open Mon–Fri 9am–1.30pm; admission fee) and displays wooden water wheels, looms, pottery, carved and painted bridal chests, lace, embroidered costumes and much else besides. Next door is the **National Struggle Museum** (open Jul–Aug Mon–Fri 8am–2pm, Sept–Jun Mon–Wed and Fri 8am–2pm, Thur 8am–2pm and 3–5.30pm; admission fee). The museum documents the EOKA armed uprising against British rule in the 1950s. On display are weapons, old newspapers and a small, red Hillman that was the command car of EOKA leader Griva Digenis. Opposite is the Pancyprian Gymnasium, a high school famous for its *enosis* activism in the 1950s.

Inside the House of Hadjigeorgakis Kornesios

It's worth strolling around this neighbourhood to see the effects of one of the restoration projects that in recent decades has been transforming parts of Old Nicosia. Formerly crumbling, the walls of the fine Ottoman-era mansions and townhouses have been shored up and painted in a variety of colours, and their interiors renovated.

Just south of the palace complex, on Odos Patriarchou Grigoriou, is the **House of Hadjigeorgakis Kornesios** (open Mon–Fri 8am–2pm; admission fee), also known as the Konak Mansion, a beautiful 18th-century structure with a Gothic-style doorway and overhanging, enclosed balcony. Restored to its original glory, and housing the **Cyprus Ethnological Museum**, the Ottoman-style interior is notable for the period furniture and carpets, as well as the ornate stairway and grand reception room. It testifies to the wealth accumulated by Kornesios, whose title *dragoman* signified that he was the official mediator between the Turkish sultan and Cypriot archbishop in the early 19th century.

Between Famagusta Gate and the Green Line is another restored Ottoman-era neighbourhood. Centred on the church of **Panagia Chrysaliniotissa** (Our Lady of the Golden Flax; open when the priest is around; admission free, donation appreciated), this tranquil area has perhaps even more characteristic period architecture than around the Archbishop's Palace.

## The Cyprus Museum

The island's finest collection of antiquities is housed in the **Cyprus Museum** (open Mon–Sat 9am–5pm, Sun 10am–1pm; admission fee) on Leoforos Mouseiou, just west of the old city. Archaeological discoveries from the Stone Age (around 7000BC) to the time of the Roman Empire are displayed here in a neoclassical building put up by the British.

Exhibits from the Bronze Age include some of the first implements made from the island's all-important copper mines, red-polished and white-painted pottery. Look out for the so-called sanctuary model (2000BC), in which worshippers and priests surround a bull sacrifice while a Peeping Tom on the sanctuary wall watches the secret ceremony.

An intriguing Mycenaean *krater* (drinking cup) imported to Egkomi by merchants from the Peloponnese in the 14th century BC has an octopus motif framing a scene of Zeus preparing warriors for battle at Troy. Nearby, a beautiful blue faïence *rhyton* (ritual anointing vessel) from the 13th century BC depicts a lively bull-hunt in Kition. Fascinating royal tomb furniture from Salamis (8th century BC) includes an ivory throne, a bed, a sword and the remains of two chariots and their horses' skeletons.

A masterpiece of Roman-Cypriot art is the monumental bronze of Emperor Septimius Severus (*circa* AD200). In contrast, behind the imperious emperor, is a movingly child-like *Sleeping Eros*. And at the far end of the hall, a marble Aphrodite is sensuous still despite lacking arms and lower legs.

A set of magnificent lions from the royal tombs at Tamassos *(see pages 35–6)* were discovered in 1997. Alongside them is a double-sided limestone stele depicting Bacchus on one side, and on the other, facing the wall, what is captioned an

## Cyprus' Terracotta Army

Perhaps the most memorable highlight of the Cyprus Museum is the 'Cyprus Terracotta Army', consisting of around 1,000 votive statues and figurines dating from between 625 and 500BC. Found at Agia Irini in northwest Cyprus, the figurines are displayed as they originally stood, around the altar of an open-air sanctuary. In a dual cult of war and fertility, soldiers, war chariots, priests with bull masks, sphinxes, Minotaurs and bulls were fashioned in all sizes, from life-size to just 10cm (4in) tall, according to their ritual importance.

'erotic scene'. Mildly erotic too is the famous *Leda and the Swan* mosaic taken from the Sanctuary of Aphrodite *(see pages 71–2)*.

Finally, look out for the gold pieces from the Lambousa Treasure Hoard and, in the last room, the small clay figures of women portrayed giving birth.

Outside the museum, you can cross the street to the shady **Municipal Gardens**, on the edge of which is the **Municipal Theatre**, the city's main venue for classical music, opera and dance, plus the Cypriot parliament's House of Representatives. Otherwise turn right on Leoforos Mouseiou, past a

*Aphrodite* at the Cyprus Museum

statue of EOKA fighter Markos Drakos throwing a grenade, towards the Pafos Gate, and beyond on Leoforos Markou Drakou to the crossing-point on the Green Line *(see page 23)*, which is at the UN's Ledra Palace Hotel checkpoint.

## Around Nicosia

The following excursions are all within 50km (30 miles) of Nicosia, making them easy day trips.

The site of **Tamassos**, an ancient city-kingdom built on copper mining, is just over 20km (12 miles) southwest of the capital, near the village of Politiko. Here excavations have uncovered a sanctuary and altar dedicated to Aphrodite, although the importance of the find is difficult for the lay person to appreciate (it seems to be nothing but knee-high rubble). Of more general interest are the two royal tombs (6th century BC). In each, stairways descend to a narrow *dromos* – a passage carved in stone to imitate wooden dwellings, complete with simulated bolted doors, window sills and 'log-roof' ceilings. A set of magnificent stone lions and sphinxes from the site are on display at the Cyprus Museum *(see page 34)*.

Nearby is the **Monastery of Agios Irakleidios** (open daily 8am–5.30pm), which is now in the hands of nuns who tend its gardens. After many restorations, the present 18th-century church houses, in a domed mausoleum, the remains of the saint who guided Paul and Barnabas on their mission to Cyprus. Herakleidos, the first bishop of Tamassos, was burned alive by unbelievers; his skull and a bone from his

At work in the fields around Tamassos

hand were salvaged and are treasured in a bejewelled gold reliquary.

Mosaic above a door at Machairas Monastery

From here it's a short journey to the **Monastery of Machairas**, 884m (2,900ft) up in the Troodos Mountains (open for groups only Mon, Tues and Thur 9am–noon; free but donation appreciated). But once you are there, the views make it all worthwhile. The monastery itself is a modern construction; an 1892 fire destroyed the original 12th-century foundation, although an allegedly miracle working icon of the Virgin Mary has survived.

The region was a natural hideout for the EOKA second in-command Gregoris Afxentiou, who died in a battle with the British near the monastery in 1957. The site of his death (a cave just below the monastery) is decorated with wreaths and is a place of pilgrimage for EOKA sympathisers.

Down the road beyond Gourri, the village of **Fikardou** represents a worthy effort to sustain Cypriot rural traditions. The whole village is protected as an Ancient Monument and has been proposed as a UNESCO World Heritage Site, with a restoration programme for its subtly coloured ironstone houses and cobbled streets. The idea is not to create another folk museum, but to revitalise the community. Alas, it does not seem to be working. In 1992, when the scheme was in its infancy, there were just eight permanent residents. It was hoped that others might be enticed by the handsome reconstruction, but the population has remained at about the same number ever since.

Asinou Church's plain exterior belies the dazzling art within

Wind your way past the church and the crumbling old buildings, scattering lizards before you, and you will discover two museum houses side by side: the **House of Katsinioros** and the **House of Achilles Dimitri** (open Jun–Aug Tue–Fri 9.30am–4.30pm, Sat 9.30am–4pm, Sun 10am–1.30pm, Sept–May Tue–Fri 9am–4pm, Sat 9am–3.30pm, Sun 10.30am–2pm; admission fee). Here, in these two houses, you can see authentic old furnishings, a spinning wheel and loom, a wine press and a brandy still.

## Asinou Church

Stranded somewhat in the middle of nowhere, outside Nikitari, 50km (31 miles) west of Nicosia, is **Panagia tis Asinou** (open daily 9.30am–5pm, Sept–Oct until 4.30pm, Nov–Apr until 4pm; free but donation appreciated), also known as Panagia Forviotissa, one of the gems of the Troodos foothills. From Nicosia take the road beyond Peristerona, then follow the signs to the 12th-century hillside church, which is famous for its magnificent Byzantine frescoes (see also page 61).

This modest but exquisite little church of ochre stone contains a veritable gallery of Byzantine art from the 12th to 16th century. A booklet explaining the different styles and subjects of the frescoes is usually available. But for a scene that is sublime beyond art, look back through the narthex to the frescoes framing the west door, open to the green wooded slope beyond. If you find the church closed go back to the village of Nikitari and search out the local priest who looks after the key.

# LARNAKA AND THE EAST

From one perspective, **Larnaka** has benefited considerably from the 1974 partition. Its airport has replaced Nicosia's as Cyprus' main port of entry, the population has more than doubled since the influx of refugees following partition, the port is reviving and resort facilities have burgeoned.

Much of northern Larnaka is built over the ancient city-kingdom of Kition. Legend attributes its founding to Kittim, a grandson of Noah, and excavated dwellings from the 2nd millennium BC make this the oldest continuously inhabited city in Cyprus. Phoenicians prospered here from the export of copper, and many centuries later Lusignan barons revived the town as a commercial and shipping centre. Under the Turks, foreign merchants and the consulates needed to protect their interests and gave the town a cosmopolitan air.

Larnaka's Agios Lazaros

## The Seafront

The palm-lined Foinikoudes (Palm Tree) Promenade is home to hotels, international restaurants, cafés and fast-food eateries. At the north end is the pleasure-boat marina. A bust of the Athenian commander Kimon, who led a fleet to recapture Kition from the Persians in 450BC (but died in the attempt), is a reminder of an ancient past.

From the marina, the dark, compacted, sandy town beach stretches almost to the old fort that marks the heart of what was the Turkish quarter. **Larnaka Fort** (open Jun–Aug Mon–Fri 9am–7.30pm, Mar–Apr and Sept–Oct daily 9am–6pm, Jan–Feb and Nov–Dec daily 9am–5pm; admission fee), built by the Turks in 1625, now houses the **Larnaka District Medieval Museum**. From the ramparts, there are good views of the harbour. Opposite is the **Cami Kebir** (Large Mosque), founded in the late 16th century and now a peaceful haven that serves Arab students and businessmen, and visiting Turkish Cypriots. Notice the tombstones topped with stone turbans in the graveyard, a rare sight so close to a mosque.

Turbanned tombstones in the Cami Kebir's graveyard

## Agios Lazaros

Inland from the mosque (at the end of Odos Dionysou), is the three-tiered campanile of the town's most revered church, **Agios Lazaros** (open daily, Apr–Aug 8am–12.30pm and 3.30–6.30pm, Sept–Mar 8am–12.30pm and 2.30––5pm; free but donation appreciated), dedicated to the man Jesus raised from the dead. According to legend, the locals of Bethany, his home town, were not much impressed by the miracle, and Lazarus was expelled in a not particularly seaworthy boat that nevertheless got him as far as Kition. Here, where he was more appreciated, Lazarus settled, became bishop and died (this time for good). The church erected over his tomb has been rebuilt many times. Its present style is a mix of extravagant Byzantine, Romanesque and Gothic styles with a fine iconostasis. The remains of Lazarus were removed from here in 890 and taken to Constantinople. In the crypt below the iconostasis you can see the empty but still much venerated sarcophagus.

## Larnaka's Museums

Opposite the marina, housed in old customs warehouses, are the **Municipal Art Gallery** (open Apr–Oct Tue–Fri 9am–1pm and 5–7pm, Sat 10am–1pm, Nov–Mar Tue–Fri 9am–1pm and 4–6pm, Sat–Sun 10am–1pm; free) and the **Tornaritis-Pierides Palaeontology Museum** (open Tue–Fri 9am–2pm, Sat–Sun 9am–noon, closed Sun June–Aug; free). They are worth a look if only to see their temporary exhibitions. Just inland is the tourist office, from where walking tours of Larnaka depart twice a week.

Across from the tourist office, on Odos Zinonos Kitieos, is the town's finest historical collection, the **Pierides Museum** (open Mon–Thur 9am–4pm, Fri–Sat 9am–1pm; admission fee). Housed in an old family mansion, which provides a charming setting, are hundreds of archaeological finds and works of art, tracing Cypriot history from neolithic to late-Byzantine times. Highlights include pottery of carved stone and red-polished clay; idols of Astarte (the Phoenician counterpart to, or forerunner of, Aphrodite); medieval glazed ceramics; Roman glassware; and Cypriot embroidery, costumes and furniture. Situated next to the museum is a sculpture garden containing several amusing avant-garde pieces.

**Larnaka District Archaeological Museum** (open Mon–Fri 9am–2.30pm, also Thur 3–5pm except Jul–Aug; admission fee) is a 10-minute walk northwest of the city centre, at

Hala Sultan Tekke, the island's most important Muslim shrine

the corner of Odos Kilkis and Odos Kimonos. Of principal interest here are the prehistoric finds from the nearby sites of Choirokoitia (*see page 44*), Kalavasos and Kition. Uphill, just beyond the museum, the paltry remains of the **Kition Acropolis**, dating back to the 13th century BC, will probably appeal only to archaeology buffs.

## West of Larnaka

About 3km (2 miles) southwest of the town, in the direction of the airport, lies the Salt Lake that provided a valuable source of income to ancient Larnaka. Lying 3m (10ft) below sea level, it is a true lake only in spring. Until recently the salt was collected each year at the end of July, after the lake dried up, but today pollution has rendered it unfit for human consumption. In autumn and winter, migratory flamingoes feed here, although their numbers have declined from several thousand to just a few hundred in recent years.

The **Hala Sultan Tekke** (open daily, June–Aug 7.30am–7.30pm, Apr–May and Sept–Oct 9am–6pm, Nov–Mar 9am–5pm; free but donation appreciated), a Muslim mosque-cum-monastery, looks like a mirage in the dry summer, thrusting its minaret through greenery and palm trees above the blinding salt flats. The shrine contains the remains of the Prophet Mohammed's aunt and foster mother, Umm Haram ('Sacred

Mother'), known as Hala Sultan in Turkish, and is thus Cyprus' most important place of Muslim pilgrimage. According to tradition, Umm Haram came to Cyprus with a party of Arab invaders in 649. Unfortunately she fell from her mule near the Salt Lake, broke her neck and was buried here. The Turks built the mosque in 1816.

The outer room has brightly painted octagonal columns and there is a gallery for women to the right. In the inner sanctuary, the guardian (who also acts as a guide) will point out the trilithon structure above Umm Haram's grave – two enormous stones about 4.5m (15ft) high, covered with a meteorite said to have come from Mt Sinai and to have hovered in the air here by itself for centuries.

Some 8km (5 miles) further is the village of Kiti and its famous church, **Panagia Angeloktisti** (open daily 8am–noon and 2–5pm; Sun until 4pm; free but donation appreciated), which literally translates as 'built by angels'. Constructed in honey-toned stone, the domed 11th-century edifice replaces a much earlier structure. Its outstanding feature is a splendid early Byzantine **mosaic** in the apse, which is among the finest works of Byzantine art in Cyprus. The standing Virgin Mary holds the Christ Child, flanked by the archangels Michael and Gabriel.

While you're in this area, you should continue through Perivolia to the coast at **Cape Kiti**. Here, several tourism developments have burgeoned on what was once a lonely, remote spot, which had not much more than a lighthouse and a medieval watch tower to mark the scenic cape.

## Red Villages

The southeast corner of Cyprus is not only a major resort area, but the island's vegetable garden. Potatoes, aubergines, tomatoes, cucumbers and onions are all grown for export in the fertile red soil of the Kokkinochoria (Red Villages) district.

## Lefkara, Choirokoitia and Stavrovouni

**Lefkara**, 40km (25 miles) west of Larnaka, is actually two villages, Pano Lefkara and Kato Lefkara, on a picturesque site in the foothills of the Troodos Mountains. Lefkara is synonymous with *lefkaritika*, the traditional embroidery that has brought the village fame for more than five centuries. Widely but incorrectly termed 'lacework', *lefkaritika* is actually linen openwork, stitched with intricate geometric patterns.

Women still work in the narrow streets and courtyards of Pano (Upper) Lefkara, patiently turning out embroidered articles which you can buy from them or in one of the many shops. A few years ago there were fewer than a dozen outlets; today there are more than 50. As a result, hustling, albeit of a mild kind, is common practice.

Smaller and mostly overlooked by the tour groups is Kato (Lower) Lefkara. It is an attractive village, with many of its traditional houses recently restored and window and door frames painted in bright Mediterranean blue.

Archaeologically inclined visitors may want to head south to **Choirokoitia**, a village tha is known for its neolithic ruins (open daily May–Aug 9am–7.30pm, Mar–Apr and Sept–Oct 9am–6pm, Nov–Feb 9am–5pm; admission fee). One of the oldest sites in Cyprus, it dates back to 5800BC. The most interesting of the four areas is the main street with its foundations of beehive-shaped houses called *tholoi*. Artefacts discovered here are on show at Nicosia's Cyprus Museum *(see page 33)*.

Lefkara is famous for intricate *lefkaritika* embroidery

On the return to Larnaka, make a detour to the famous mountain-top monastery of **Stavrovouni** (Mountain of the Cross; open daily, Apr–Aug 8am–noon and 3–6pm, Sept–Mar 8am–noon and 2–5pm; free but donation appreciated; men only), which sits just off the road to Nicosia. At an altitude of 689m (2,260ft), it has an unbeatable view from its isolated perch north to Nicosia and the hazy Pentadaktylos Mountains, and south over terraced hills to the Salt Lake, Larnaka and the sea.

Stavrovouni was built on the site of a shrine to Aphrodite which, like the monastery today, was off-limits

The church at the mountain-top monastery of Stavrovouni

to women. Nevertheless, Helena, mother of Emperor Constantine, is said to have ventured up here in AD330 to found the monastery and endow it with a piece of the True Cross. The relic is still proudly displayed in the monastery church. Note that cameras are forbidden anywhere in the grounds.

At the foot of the winding road up to Stavrovouni is the **Monastery of Agia Varvara** (St Barbara), open in the morning and late afternoon (closed noon–3pm). Over the road is the **studio of Brother Kallinikos**. He is world-renowned as one of the best contemporary icon painters in the Orthodox Church. It is fascinating to watch the elderly monk at work in his chaotic studio, where some of his icons are for sale.

## East to Agia Napa

Just beyond the resort hotels east of Larnaka, you pass through the British Sovereign Base Area of **Dhekelia**. Here the Greek-Cypriot territory is squeezed into a narrow strip by the border of the Turkish-occupied zone. East of Dhekelia is **Potamos**, a picturesque creek that's invariably jammed with small, gaily painted fishing boats, flanked by a couple of authentic seafood tavernas.

In the years following the Turkish occupation of Famagusta, **Agia Napa** was transformed from a tiny fishing village into Cyprus' major resort. Indeed, in recent years it has become one of the Mediterranean's best-known dance-club destinations *(see page 91)*. As you enter the town, its character is evident from the international bars, restaurants and seaside souvenir shops, but the change is most pronounced in the square around the **Monastery of Agia Napa** (Our Lady of the Forest; open daily dawn–dusk; free). Today, apart from a sycamore said to be 600 years old, the only forest is that of the concrete pillars and neon signs that mark the island's largest concentration of bars and nightclubs.

However, during the day (when the clubbers are asleep or at the beach), the square and monastery are peaceful. The monastery,

On the beach at Agia Napa

built around 1530, remains one of Cyprus' most handsome Venetian buildings, with an octagonal marble fountain in the Gothic cloister. It is now a conference centre for the World Council of Churches, and its church is only open regularly for Sunday services.

Another cultural attraction of note is the **Thalassa Municipal Museum of the Sea** (open June–Sept Tue–Sun 9am–2pm, 6–10pm, Oct–May Tue–Sat 9am–5pm, Sun 10am–2pm; admission fee), next door to the tourist office. It contains shells, fossils and taxidermic marine specimens and a replica of the ancient Kyrenia ship *(see page 79)*.

Agia Napa's growth is largely a result of its fine beaches of golden sand, a rarity in Cyprus. The main one is **Nissi Beach**, a picture-postcard strip and cove with limpid blue waters and a tiny island within paddling distance. At nearby **Makronisos**, another popular beach, there are 19 rock tombs dating from the classical and Hellenistic periods.

## Cape Gkreko

For anyone who can't quite see the point of staying up all night in the clubs of Agia Napa, there's **Cape Gkreko**, the island's southeastern tip, where spectacular rocky inlets, caves and bays provide an escape from the crowds.

Head east on the coast road towards the cape and just outside Agia Napa, beside the Grecian Bay Hotel, you'll find the

---

### Varosha boat trip

An intriguing boat trip from Agia Napa goes past the Green Line as far as Famagusta to view the decaying town of Varosha. Once a major resort, it has been left to rot since 1974, when it was declared UN territory (though it is policed by the Turkish army). Now that travel to the North has been eased, you can also drive around Varosha's outskirts on the Famagusta side, but you still can't enter or take pictures.

A view of the coast near Cape Gkreko

**Thalassines Spilies**, sea caves famous for a much-photographed sea arch and frequented by snorkellers and divers. A few kilometres further along the main road are the more spectacular **Palatia (Palace) Caves**.

Further still is the **Cape Gkreko viewpoint**. You will have to walk the last 500m (1,600ft) uphill, but it is well worth the effort. From an altitude of almost 100m (330ft), the clifftop view looking west is stupendous. Just to the east is **Cape Gkreko** itself. The point is occupied by transmitters belonging to Radio Monaco International and is off-limits .

Heading north will bring you to **Konnos Bay**, probably the most picturesque sandy cove in all of Cyprus. On a quiet day, it can be heaven. In midsummer, Agia Napa 'booze cruises' (or 'orgy boats') and their sound systems disturb the peace.

The coast road continues north to the lovely sandy beaches of Fig Tree Bay, around which the characterless resort of **Protaras** has sprung up.

# LIMASSOL AND THE SOUTH COAST

**Limassol** (*Lemesos* in Greek) is Cyprus' good-time town, with plush restaurants and a brash and boisterous nightlife. Fittingly, it plays host to the island's most exuberant pre-Lenten Carnival. However, many visitors see relatively little of the city itself, as most accommodation is away from the centre in a strip of high-rise hotels 5–10km (3–6 miles) east.

It was at Limassol that the crusading English king Richard the Lionheart stopped off in 1191. He defeated the tyrannical Byzantine usurper Isaac Comnenos, then proceeded to sell off Cyprus – first to the Knights Templar (who settled in Limassol), and then to the Lusignans *(see page 16)*. The crusader Knights of St John made Limassol their headquarters in 1291, when the town flourished as never before.

By the early 19th century, earthquakes and the rapacity of the Genoese and Turks had reduced the city to a crumbling village. British development of the wine industry breathed new life into it and, since the 1974 partition, Limassol's population has increased by 50 percent to more than 150,000, second to that of Nicosia.

The solitary surviving monument to the town's feudal glory is **Limassol Castle**, an imposing, 13th-century stone fortification near the old port. Today it houses the **Cyprus Medieval Museum** (open Mon–Sat 9am–5pm, Sun 10am–1pm; admission fee), the island's best collection from this period, with some well-preserved tombstones, and suits of armour

Modern sculpture on display at Limassol's seafont

View of Limassol's rooftops from the castle battlements

that reflect the local metal-working tradition. The building itself is also interesting and has fine views from the battlements.

The area around the castle is particularly pleasant, with tropical gardens and a clutch of attractive pavement cafés and historic buildings. The narrow lanes around here used be the Turkish commercial quarter. You can enter the **Cami Kabir** mosque, which lies a few metres from the castle and is still used by Limassol's Arab population and Muslim visitors, among them now Turkish Cypriots from the North. Behind it, you can peer into excavations of an older mosque. There's a working Turkish bath *(hamam)* nearby.

As you wander around this interesting quarter, you will see artisans' workshops, often quite primitive, where the speciality is metalware (particularly copper and tin). A carob mill and warehouse here, dating from the early 1900s, has been restored and transformed into a cultural and shopping centre with restaurants and cafés.

It is just 1.5km (1 mile) along the seafront promenade from the old port to the **municipal gardens**, a pleasant place to rest for a while. There's also a miniature 'zoo' here that contains mostly birds. At the far end of the gardens, the small, modern **Limassol District Archaeological Museum** (Mon–Fri 9am–5pm, Sat 10am–1pm; admission fee) contains some fascinating archaeological treasures, among them jewellery and expressive terracotta figurines. There's a beautiful head of Aphrodite from Kourion as well as a massive statue of the Egyptian god Bes from ancient Amathous *(see page 52)*.

From the gardens, it's a 10-minute walk back towards the port along Odos Agiou Andreou to the **Folk Art Museum** (June–Sept Mon–Fri 8.30am–1.30pm and 4–6.30pm, Thur am only, Oct–May Mon–Fri 8.30am–1.30pm and 3–5.30pm, Thur am only; admission fee). It provides a glimpse of rural Cypriot life through wood-carving, embroidery, jewellery-making and weaving.

Wine-making in Cyprus is not only an industry but also a tourist attraction, so you should find a visit to a **winery** both instructive and enjoyable. The top wineries, Keo, Etko and Sodap, cluster together on Leoforos Fragklinou Rousvelt, a 10-minute walk west of the castle. All offer short tours which usually begin at 9.30 or 10am and always end with a tasting.

Stone carvings in the Folk Art Museum

East of town, hidden among the beach resort hotels, are the fenced-off ruins of the agora of **Amathous** (open daily, June–Aug 9am–7.30pm, Apr–May and Sept–Oct 9am–6pm, Nov–Mar 9am–5pm; admission fee), one of the island's oldest city-kingdoms. The fragmentary remains are likely to be of interest only to experts.

A few kilometres further on is **Governor's Beach**, a dark-sand beach which in recent years has been the focus of hotel and villa developments. A local bus connects it with Limassol.

## West of Limassol

Traces of the earliest human presence on the island – hunters of pygmy hippos from 9000BC – were found on the **Akrotiri Peninsula** west of Limassol. Half of the peninsula is made up of salt lake – more flats than lake – popular with migratory birds, notably pink flamingoes, from October to March. Most of the remainder of the peninsula is occupied by the airfield and other installations of a British Sovereign Base Area.

Just south of Akrotiri village, a bumpy track leads east to **Agios Nikolaos ton Gaton** (St Nicholas of the Cats; open daily; free). The fame of the monastery has everything to do with the snake-hunting cats its monks reared; today's institution is a modern building with little of historical or architectural interest, run by a handful of nuns.

North of the peninsula, the impressive 15th-century keep of **Kolossi Castle** (open daily, June–Aug 9am–7.30pm, Apr–May and Sept–Oct 9am–6pm, Nov–Mar 9am–5pm; admission fee) is one of the icons of Cypriot tourism. Once the headquarters of the Knights of St John, from here they administered their considerable sugar plantations and vineyards. The *Commanderie*, as the headquarters was known, gave its name to their prized Commandaria dessert wine, still produced today.

Among the rooms, all now empty, the one with a huge fireplace was the kitchen. In the adjacent room is a damaged fresco, the only surviving decoration. Climb the steep, narrow spiral staircase for the view from the battlements. Outside you can see traces of an ancient aqueduct and an imposing Gothic structure that served as a sugar refinery.

## Kourion

Before exploring the great archaeological site of Kourion, stop in the nearby village of Episkopi to do a little homework at the **Kourion Archaeological Museum** (open Mon–Fri 9am–2.30pm, Sept–July also Thur 3–5pm; admission fee), which holds dramatic finds from the earthquake that devastated Kourion in AD365. On display is a touching group of three human skeletons: archaeologists believe them to be of a 25-year-old male protecting a 19-year-old female with an 18-month-old baby clutched to her breast. Other exhibits include a Roman stone lion fountain, terracotta vases and figurines.

Kourion's Roman theatre

The House of the Gladiators

Just west of Episkopi is **Kourion** itself (open daily, June–Aug 8am–7.30pm, Apr–May and Sept–Oct, 8am–6pm, Nov–Mar 8am–5pm; admission fee). Along with Salamis in the north *(see page 82)*, it is the island's most important archaeological site. Not the least of its attractions is its spectacular setting high on a bluff above Episkopi Bay. In ancient times, sacrilegious criminals were hurled to their death on to the rocks below.

Experts attribute the foundation of the town to Mycenaean settlers in the 13th century BC. Known as Curium to the Romans, it converted to Christianity in the 4th century, with its faith sorely tested by a devastating earthquake in 365. After Arab raids in the 7th century, the bishopric moved out to what is now Episkopi, leaving Kourion to sink into oblivion.

The site is large. Your first stop is the reconstructed **Roman theatre** (AD50–175), occupying a spectacular site on the edge of the bluff. The theatre once seated 3,500 and is used today for various open-air performances.

Behind the theatre is the Roman **Villa of Eustolios**. The floor mosaics of birds and fish indicate that Eustolios was a man of wealth and taste; inscriptions to both Apollo and Christ suggest that, at least from a religious perspective, he was prudent enough to hedge his bets. Eustolios later added a bathhouse, which he opened to destitute survivors of the earthquake, as attested by an inscription. The central room features some more remarkable mosaics, including one of a partridge and another of Ktisis, a deity who personifies creation.

The extensive ruins of the city include the *agora* (market-place) and *nymphaeum* (fountain house). Unfortunately, this area is likely to be inaccessible as excavations continue. Turn to the left to explore the remains of an early Christian **basilica**. The basilica's plan reveals 12 pairs of granite columns for the nave. To the north is the baptistry, where congregants disrobed and were anointed with oil before descending to the font.

Opposite are the ruins of a colonnaded portico paved with the so-called **Achilles mosaic**. It depicts Achilles, disguised as a woman to avoid enlistment in the expedition to Troy, being tricked by Odysseus into grabbing a spear and shield and revealing his identity. The nearby **House of the Gladiators** is so named for its mosaics of two duels, one with an aristocratic looking referee – perhaps the owner of the house.

The remains of a public bathhouse

The Sanctuary of Apollo Ylatis

On the main road about 1km (½ mile) west of the main site are the scant remains of the city's ancient **stadium**, where athletes performed on a U-shaped track before 6,000 spectators.

The **Sanctuary of Apollo Ylatis** (God of the Woodland; open daily, June–Aug 9am–7.30pm, Apr–May and Sept–Oct 9am–6pm, Nov–Mar 9am–5pm; admission fee) is to the west. Apollo was worshipped here as early as the 8th century BC, but most of the present structures were put up around AD100, and destroyed in the earthquake of 365.

From the guardian's lodge, take the path west to the pilgrims' entrance (through the stumpy remains of the Pafos Gate). The buildings here were probably hostels and storehouses for worshippers' votive offerings. The surplus was carefully placed in the *vothros* pit (at the centre of the site), which was full of terracotta figurines, mostly horse riders – still intact when uncovered by the archaeologists. Follow the path along the sanctuary's main street to the Temple of Apollo, which has been partially reconstructed to look as it did in AD100.

## West to Aphrodite's Birthplace

If the flat, hard-packed sands of Curium Beach don't appeal to you, try the coarse sand and shingle of Avdimou Beach, about 10km (6 miles) further west. But if you crave the creature comforts of a resort, then continue on to **Pissouri**. Note that the signs you see to both Avdimou and Pissouri are to the inland villages, not the beaches; follow instead the signs for Avdimou Beach or Pissouri Bay, which later changes to 'K. Pissouri' (short for Kato, or Lower Pissouri), then finally to 'Pissouri Jetty'. The latter is an attractive, sheltered place, with a coarse sand-and-shingle beach.

It is easy to be sceptical about a few rocks in the sea that are claimed to be the birthplace of a goddess, but this stretch of coast and the **Petra tou Romiou** rock formation, better known as **Aphrodite's Birthplace**, is a beautiful natural feature. (The Greek name, 'Rock of Romios', has nothing to do with Aphrodite, but commemorates the Byzantine hero Romios.) He must also have been endowed with supernatural powers, as he is said to have used the huge rocks as missiles to ward off pirates. The views east, away from the rocks to the dazzling white cliffs, are spectacular. Opposite the rocks, there is a parking and café. The water here is clear and inviting.

Petra tou Romiou, where Aphrodite first emerged from the sea

# TROODOS MOUNTAINS

➤ The **Troodos Mountains** in central Cyprus are the island's principal upland (note that it is pronounced more 'tro-dos', than 'true-doss'). They provide many things: a breath of fresh air for hot and flustered visitors and locals, a splendid collection of tiny Byzantine churches scattered around the hillsides, wonderful walking trails and, most importantly, much of the island's fresh water.

The roads climb through foothills with rushing streams and orchards, past villages perched on the slopes, surrounded at higher altitudes by pine forest. Monks and Greek-Cypriot EOKA fighters have also found refuge here, and the monasteries are now joined by resort hotels and spas, with even a little winter skiing near the resort of Troodos. On the southern slopes, above the 1,000-metre (3,300-ft) line, are the vineyards and

Typical village in the Troodos Mountains

villages that produce Cyprus' highly regarded, sweet red dessert wine, Commandaria.

## Platres to Troodos

At an altitude of 1,128m (3,700ft), **Pano Platres** makes a good base for visiting the whole Troodos region. The little town occupies a charming and shady mountain site and features several hotels, restaurants and shops. The most popu-

Moufflon, or wild mountain sheep, thrive in the Troodos

lar pastime here is walking, and the Cyprus Tourism Organisation has marked several walking trails in the mountains, aimed at most ability levels. Stop at the Platres office for details. The most popular excursion here is the 2-km (1-mile) walk to the pretty **Kalidonia Falls**. The walk starts at the Psilo Dhendro restaurant and trout farm just outside Platres *(see page 140)*, and is well marked.

Some 4km (2½ miles) from Platres is **Foini**, famous for its red-clay ceramics. You can see this craft being practised at home by a couple of local women who will be happy to let you watch them work. Foini also has a fine folklore museum.

**Omodos**, renovated as a Troodos showpiece village, lies 6km (4 miles) south of Foini. It's an attractive place, but has become over-commercialised, and the tour buses diminish the atmosphere their occupants have come to savour. However, you can still find peace and quiet in the **Monastery of Timiou Stavrou** (True Cross), which contains a memorial to EOKA.

It seems that all roads in the mountains lead to the eponymous resort of **Troodos**, which at 1,676m (5,500ft) is the island's highest. In the winter it has decent ski slopes, while

Old Kakopetria

in spring and autumn, it's a good starting point for dedicated ramblers. Avoid midsummer when its main street turns into an overcrowded promenade of kitsch stalls and rumbling tour buses. A **visitor centre**, near the Dolphin restaurant, helps orientate visitors to the high mountains, and provides maps and information on the local wildlife and plants.

Less committed mountaineers may prefer to take a drive above the town to Cyprus' tallest peak, **Mt Olympos** (1,951m/6,401ft). For security reasons, you have to walk the last few hundred metres up to the giant British 'golf ball' radar installation on the summit; and the views are not that great. It's much better to gird your loins and tackle one of two nature trails – the Atalante or the Artemis – that circle the summit.

## Kakopetria

In recent years, the Cyprus government has been investing in the reconstruction of traditional village houses as part of its plan to staunch the population flow from the hill villages to the coastal resorts and towns. And in few places is this effort more to be admired than in old **Kakopetria**. This historic part of town is more or less one long narrow street that runs parallel to the leafy river. The houses with balconies are being restored to bring out the subtle russet, amber and silver hues of the local stone and, with their log-cabin stores, have a real alpine feel. The town's tour de force is its beautifully restored **wooden mill**. The upper floor of the old flour mill is now home to The Mill restaurant *(see page 139)*, while the rest of the building has been turned into a hotel.

Just outside the village is one of the Troodos Mountains' famous frescoed churches *(see below)*, **Agios Nikolaos tis Stegis** (open Tue–Sat 9am–4pm, Sun 11am–4pm; free but donation appreciated). The name translates as St Nicholas of the Roof, and refers to the upper roof of shingles, which was built in the 13th century to shelter the older domed roof of tiles. Inside, the oldest frescoes date from the church's foundation in the 11th century.

## Frescoed Churches

The Troodos Mountains' remarkable painted churches were built mostly between the 11th and the 16th centuries. For visitors, the astonishing degree of preservation and the striking beauty of the artwork makes for compulsive viewing. For scholars, the churches provide a fascinating lesson on the history of sacred art, a fact that has been officially recognised by UNESCO (10 Troodos churches are on their World Cultural Heritage list). But it's also worth remembering that the primary function of the art was to act as a religious cartoon strip, teaching the simple, illiterate and often isolated parishioners the lessons of the Gospels.

The finest concentration of painted churches is in the northeastern part of the Troodos, where Panagia tis Asinou Church *(see page 38)*, Agios Nikolaos tis Stegis (in Kakopetria), Panagia tis Podithou (in Galata) and the outstanding Panagia tou Araka (in Lagoudera) are all within a short drive of each other. If a church is closed, you will have to trace the key-holder, usually the parish priest. Details are sometimes posted on the church door; otherwise try the nearest café.

Off the eastern edge of the Troodos, at Palaichori, you'll find the latest addition to the roster of UNESCO mountain churches, **Metamorfosis tou Sotiros** (Transfiguration of the Saviour; no fixed opening times; admission free but donation appreciated), dating from the early 16th-century. Among its frescoes is a fine representation of the transfiguration of Jesus.

## Galata

Just north of Kakopetria, **Galata** has a UNESCO-listed 16th-century church. Heading north out of town, drive slowly and you will spot **Panagia Podithou** (open daily 10am–1pm and 2–5pm; free, donation appreciated). It is not as well preserved, nor is the artwork as detailed as at some Troodos churches, but it still has some outstanding images. If it is closed the key-holder is usually somewhere between here and the smaller church of Archangelos, also known as **Panagia Theotokos**, nearby. In Galata itself there is a small folk-art museum and a restored Ottoman *han* (inn).

Frescoed dome in the church at Lagoudera

If you've developed a taste for these mountain churches, continue east to **Lagoudera**, where you will find **Panagia tou Araka**, another fine example, with frescoes dating from 1192.

Heading in the opposite direction, the road west from Troodos winds through pine groves, vineyards and orchards of apples, pears, peaches, cherries, almonds and walnuts to **Prodromos**, 1,400m (4,600ft) above sea level. Its modest hotels and restaurants are popular with hikers and jeep safaris. Further on is **Pedoulas**, famous for its cherries. In spring the locals flock here to see thousands of trees in blossom.

## West to Kykkos

**Kykkos Monastery** (monastery: open daily dawn–dusk; free but donation appreciated; museum: open daily, June–Oct 10am–6pm, Nov–May 10am–4pm; admission fee), 20km (12 miles) from Pedoulas, sits proudly remote from the world on a mountainside surrounded by pine forest. The drive offers marvellous views of the mountains at every twist and turn.

Kykkos (Panagia tou Kykkou) is the richest and most important monastery on the island. Founded in 1094 by a hermit, it grew in prestige when Emperor Alexis Comnenos gave it a rich land grant and an icon of the Virgin Mary said to have been painted by St Luke. Having survived several fires, the icon is now covered in gilded silver. Its legendary rain-making powers still bring in farmers to pray in times of drought. Offerings left here range from jewellery to simple *ex votos* of beeswax.

If you come at a busy time, you may be dismayed to see a long slow-moving queue of people waiting to enter the church. These will be Cypriots who wish to pass directly in front of the iconostasis, kissing the images to show their piety. Other visitors can simply go straight into the church via the rear door. The general reaction on experiencing the intense glitter and

Kykkos Monastery

exuberant ornamentation of the church is one of astonishment. In fact, apart from the precious icon and a few other pieces, there is little of historical or significant artistic value here, but for the lay visitor this hardly matters.

The monastery has been levelled by fire on four occasions; the first occurred in 1365, the last in 1813, so its buildings are no older than the early 19th century. Recently, they have been covered by scores of glittering new mosaics, though the real jewel in the crown is the excellent museum. Here in cool and calm, you can learn about the history of the foundation and see some of its finest treasures.

Kykkos is also famous for having had Archbishop Makarios among its novices (he is buried on a hill above the monastery). In the 1950s, Kykkos was reputed to have served as a communications and supply base for the EOKA movement, and so became a symbol of the Cypriot nationalist struggle (see page 21). On the road to the monastery, you will see brown-and-white tourist signs pointing to old EOKA hideouts.

West of Kykkos, rough mountain tracks and hard-surfaced roads lead downhill into the **Pafos Forest** and pass through **Cedar Valley**, one of the highlights of the island's reforestation project. This steep-sided ravine hosts some 50,000 indigenous cedar trees (Cedrus brevifolia) and, in the surrounding forests of the rugged **Tripilos-Mavroi Gremmoi Nature Reserve**, the formerly endangered Cypriot wild mountain sheep, the moufflon, roam free.

# PAFOS AND THE WEST

**Pafos** has been transformed in a few decades from a sleepy fishing port into a booming resort town. But visitors who want more than just sun and sand have plenty to occupy them. Pafos was the island's original capital and has a wealth of historic sites. It is also a good base for exploring nearby mountain villages and the nature trails of the Akamas Peninsula.

Legend attributes the founding of Palaia (Old) Pafos to the priest-king Cinyras, and the city-kingdom gained renown as the centre of Aphrodite's cult. The last king of Palaia Pafos, Nicocles, established the port of Nea (New) Pafos in the 4th century BC, though Palaia Pafos remained the centre of Aphrodite worship until the 4th century AD. Within 100 years of its founding, Nea Pafos surpassed Salamis as the chief city of Cyprus. However, earthquakes in 332 and 342 and Arab

Fishing boats in Pafos harbour

attacks in the 7th century forced most of the population inland to Ktima. For centuries, Pafos languished as a miserable, unsanitary seaport. However, the population gradually rose to over 2,000 by the late 19th century. It continued to grow and prosper, and in spite of some damage during the 1974 war, it bounced back; the explosion of development after the opening in 1985 of Pafos International Airport attracted not only tourists but also new Cypriot settlers.

## Kato Pafos

Kato (Lower) Pafos, along the seaside, is where most visitors stay, and is heavily developed. But the harbour still provides a picturesque haven for fishing and sailing boats as it curves around a jetty to the old **Pafos Fort** (open daily, June–Aug 10am–6pm, Sept–May 10am–5pm; admission fee). Over the centuries, the fort has been a feudal castle, Turkish tower and British salt warehouse (scattered remains of an earlier Roman and Byzantine fort lie nearby). It's now an empty shell but worth the entrance fee for its rooftop views.

Just across the harbour car park are several of Pafos' ancient monuments. The

first, identified by its trademark arch, is the ruin that's
known as **Saranda Kolones**
(40 columns), named after
the number of granite
columns found lying around
here. Excavations have established its identity as a
French crusader castle built at
the end of the 12th century
and destroyed by an earthquake in 1222.

The ruins of Saranda Kolones

With the harbour on your
left, walk towards the large, modern shed-like building in the
distance. Sheltered beneath are the famous **Pafos Mosaics**
(open daily, June–Aug 8am–7.30pm, Sept–May 8am–5pm;
admission fee). These splendid decorative floors were uncovered in the remains of luxurious Roman villas (3rd century
AD) of Nea Pafos and constitute the most important group of
mosaics in Cyprus. The 'houses' are named after the mosaics'
most prominent motifs. The **House of Dionysos** displays the
god of wine returning from India on a chariot drawn by two
panthers. This and other scenes, such as Dionysos counselling
moderation to the nymph Akme drinking wine from a bowl,
and King Icarios of Athens getting shepherds drunk with their
first taste of wine, were customary decorations for the dining
room. The **House of Aion** has a spectacular five-panelled mosaic. Its large central panel depicts Aion, god of eternity, judging a beauty contest between a smug-looking Queen
Cassiopeia (the winner) and the unhappy, prettier Nereides
water nymphs. There are two more villas open to the public,
the **Villa of Theseus** and the **House of Orpheus**.

A short walk north leads to the restored **Odeon**, a small
amphitheatre dating from the 2nd century AD, built entirely

Pafos is famed for its Roman mosaics

of hewn limestone blocks. In a picturesque hillside setting, it seats 1,250 spectators for the musical and theatrical performances held regularly in the summer.

## Kato Pafos to Ktima

From the road entrance to the harbour, Leoforos Apostolou Pavlou climbs towards the excavated site of a 4th-century AD Christian basilica known as **Agia Kyriaki**. Amid the ruins of the seven-aisled church, you can make out mosaic pavements with floral and geometric patterns, Corinthian capitals and columns of green-and-white marble imported from Greece. Arabic graffiti on the columns dates from the invasion that destroyed the basilica in 653. One of the columns is called **St Paul's Pillar**, to which the apostle was (apocryphally) tied and lashed 39 times for preaching the Gospel.

Amid the ruins is the handsome post-Byzantine **Panagia Chrysopolitissa** church (sometimes also referred to, confusingly, as Agia Kyriaki). Just to the north of the site are tiny, ruined, twin-domed Turkish baths, with an ancient gnarled tree pushing up through the masonry.

A little further up the hill is the intriguing sight of a tree festooned with hundreds of handkerchiefs and rags. It marks the **Catacomb of Agia Solomoni**, once regarded as a spot where disease could be cured by miracles, and still doing a good trade with believers if today's votive offerings in the tiny rock-cut chapel below are anything to go by. The tradition of tying a handkerchief to a tree at a sacred site is common in the Near and Middle East. The handkerchief is given as a votive offering (akin to lighting a candle in a church in the West to accompany a prayer of thanks or devotion), and goes back to the days when handkerchiefs were valuable items.

Northwest of what was Nea Pafos is the ancient community's necropolis, known as the **Tombs of the Kings** (open daily, June–Aug 8am–7.30pm, Apr–May and Sept–Oct 8am–6pm, Nov–Mar 8am–5pm; admission fee). The title is a misnomer, as the subterranean burial chambers were built from the 3rd century BC to the 3rd century AD, when Pafos had no kings. But many of the tombs are imposing enough to suggest they were at least the resting places of important officials. This 'city of the dead' is an imitation of the city of the living, thus giving an insight into the architecture of Nea Pafos: spacious courtyards with Doric columns and decorative entablatures. It is fun to explore (tombs 3, 4 and 8 are the best), but do be careful as there are unprotected drops.

Within the Tombs of the Kings

## Ktima

Set on a hilltop above the resort, the upper part of Pafos known as **Ktima** is a breath of fresh air and everyday reality. There is a colourful daily produce market and a variety of souvenir stalls. After shopping, you can sit down for a drink or a meal and enjoy the excellent views of the coast.

There are two small museums in the centre of Ktima. The **Ethnographical Museum**, also known as the Eliades Collection, on Odos Exo Vrisis (open Mon–Sat 9.30am–5pm, Sun 10am–2pm; admission fee), is set in a charming 19th-century house. It combines prehistoric fossils, classical antiquities and Cypriot folklore of the 18th and 19th centuries. In the garden, burial chambers from the 3rd century BC have been uncovered. Across the road, in a wing of the **Bishop's Palace**, is the **Byzantine Museum** (open Mon–Fri 9am–4pm, Sat 9am–1pm; admission fee), a gallery of icons salvaged from local chapels.

You'll need transport to reach the **Pafos District Archaeological Museum** (open Mon–Fri 9am–5pm, Sat 10am–1pm; admission fee), which is on the road to Limassol. It houses some remarkable sculptures found in the Villa of Theseus *(see page 67)*. They include a statue of Asclepios (the Greek master of medicine) feeding an egg to the snake coiled around his staff. Also, look out for the pottery hot-water bottles from the 1st century AD, specially moulded to fit all parts of the body.

## South of Pafos

Just southeast of Pafos is the village of **Geroskipou**, which means the 'Sacred Garden' of Aphrodite. Pilgrims would stop here on their way to the goddess's temple at Palaia Pafos; today, they stop to buy pottery souvenirs or Cypriot Delight, which are made at several roadside outlets.

The 11th-century church of **Agia Paraskevi** in Geroskipou is a rare island example of a five-domed basilica. Inside are some 15th century murals and a much-revered icon from the same period, with a *Virgin and Child* on one side and a *Crucifixion* on the reverse.

In a restored house nearby is the informative **Museum of Folk Art** (open July–Aug Mon–Fri 7.30am–2.30pm, Sept–June Mon–Wed and Fri 7am–2.30pm, Thur 7.30am–6pm; admission fee). Typical of a rich Cypriot's villa in the 18th century, it has an upper storey ringed with handsome wooden balconies. Displays include elaborate gourds made into unlikely items (such as swimming aids for children), domestic and farming implements, rural costumes, furniture and heirlooms.

From here, continue going southeast for about 12km (8 miles) and turn off at **Kouklia**, once Palaia Pafos, where the cult of Aphrodite was celebrated. As described by Homer, the rites of the love goddess flourished here at the **Sanctuary of Aphrodite** (open daily 9am–4pm; admission fee). Alas, little romance can be found in the ruins. Most of the valuable finds have been taken to Nicosia, though a copy of the famous mosaic of *Leda and the Swan* remains in situ. The sturdy Château de Covocle (originally a Lusignan manor-farm) is now home to the **Palaia Pafos Museum** (same hours as the Sanctuary; free). Its prize

Remains of fluted columns at the Sanctuary of Aphrodite

exhibit is a large conical stone that symbolised the goddess (her beauty was too great to represent literally) and was the epicentre of Aphrodite worship.

## North of Pafos

The beaches in Pafos are unremarkable, so it's no surprise that many visitors travel 10km (6 miles) north to the better sands, plentiful watersports, and beachside dining of the bustling **Coral Bay** resort. A wave of development has all but filled the once extensive olive groves, orchards and banana plantations between here and the old hilltop village of **Pegeia** with undistinguished modern villas. Further up the coast, the handsome little fishing harbour at **Agios Georgios**, crowned by a clifftop church and an archaeological zone, seems to be going the same way.

To the northeast, 10km (6 miles) from Pafos, the **Monastery of Agios Neofytos** dominates a wooded slope (open daily, Apr–Oct 9am–1pm and 2–6pm, Nov–Mar 9am–1pm and 2–4pm; admission fee). Its church has fine frescoes and icons, but the main focus is the 12th-century **Enkleistra** (Hermitage), around which the monastery grew. The saintly historian and theologian Neofytos (1134–1214) supposedly hacked this cave-dwelling out of the rock with his own hands and then supervised the wonderful frescoes that decorate the chapel and cell. One shows Neofytos himself, flanked by archangels Michael and Gabriel.

On the north coast, the handsome small town of **Polis** stands where the ancient city-kingdom of Mari-

Monastery of Agios Neofytos

The rugged landscape of the Akamas Peninsula

on once boasted rich gold and copper mines. Some of the best archaeological finds from the site are on display here at the **Marion-Arsinoë Archaeological Museum** (open Mon–Wed and Fri 8am–2pm, Thur 9am–5pm (8am–2pm July–Aug), Sat 9am–5pm; admission fee). The town centre itself has been attractively restored and has a pleasant if rather touristy enclave of cafés and restaurants. Polis is a prelude to the fishing port and beach resort of **Lakki**. Restaurants, cafés and bars cluster around Lakki's picturesque harbour, flanked by sand and pebble beaches. The harbour itself is the watery gateway to the Akamas Peninsula.

Romantics should head west along the peninsula until the road ends at the car park of the **Loutra tis Afroditis** (Baths of Aphrodite). From here it's an easy five-minute walk to a small, shaded natural pool and springs set in a cool green glade, where our local heroine used to bathe to rejuvenate herself. Mere mortals are not allowed to cool off here, but on the other side of the car park, a path leads down to a couple of narrow pebble beaches with crystal-clear shallow water. Alternatively, if you want to go hiking, marked paths lead off into the peninsula from Aphrodite's Baths.

➤   The rest of the **Akamas Peninsula** is pristine, one of the few unspoilt wildernesses left on the island and currently a major battleground between environmentalists and developers *(see below)*. In the protected **Lara Bay Marine Reserve**, on the peninsula's west coast, endangered green and loggerhead turtles come ashore to bury their eggs. Despite the threat of development elsewhere on the peninsula, the government has decided, so far at least, that this beach will remain untouched.

## A Wilderness Under Threat

Untamed and scenic, the Akamas Peninsula arouses strong passions, both among those who admire this pristine wilderness for its beauty and wildlife, and among developers who see it as a potential paradise for upmarket tourists. Hikers, birdwatchers and nature-lovers relish the Akamas' rugged terrain. It is the last major piece of unspoilt coastline in South Cyprus. But commercial interests are encroaching, and there are proposals for luxury hotels, and even a heliport.

Organisations as disparate as the World Bank, the European Union, Friends of the Earth and Greenpeace have called for the creation of a national park. The island's powerful developer lobby and some local residents oppose this, or at any rate prefer to have only limited protection for the area for around 20 years. In 2000, a government committee recommended 'mild and controlled' development in the Akamas and to reduce the area of the proposed national park by more than two-thirds.

The intense debate continues. Recently, the Cyprus government has – yet again – declared its intention to establish a national park, but still is providing no details. Meanwhile, commercial development, both legal and illegal, continues to encroach on the peninsula.

# NORTHERN CYPRUS

The Turkish-occupied north, which comprises around 37 percent of the island, contains some of Cyprus' most beautiful landscapes, best beaches, most dramatic historical sites and two of its finest towns. Partition and the subsequent political isolation helped preserve the countryside from the ravages of mass tourism, something that is evident at the fine golden-sand beaches of Famagusta.

It is possible to whizz around Northern Cyprus in a day and cover – or at least glimpse – all the main sights, although unless you are short on time, this is not recommended. In three days you can see the sights, including northern Nicosia, at a more leisurely pace.

## Northern Nicosia

Compared with the thriving southern half of the city, north ern Nicosia is quieter and poorer but, as with much of the North, this has begun to change. From the Ledra Palace Hotel checkpoint, once the sole and now one of five buffer-zone crossing-points *(see page 77 for entry requirements)*, walk along Sarayönü Sokagi to **Atatürk Meydanı**, the hub of Turkish Nicosia. At its centre is a granite column probably brought from Salamis by the Venetians.

Venetian coat of arms on Atatürk Meydanı

From the square, head north along Girne Caddesi to the **Mevlevi Tekke** (open daily, summer 9am–2pm, winter 9am–1pm and 2–4.45pm; admission fee). This

Selimiye Mosque

was once a ceremonial hall used by the Mevlevi whirling dervish sect, outlawed in 1925. The multi-domed, 17th-century building now has a small Turkish **Ethnographical Museum** with a reconstruction of the whirling dervishes' dance floor complete with mannequins (sadly static). The building itself is the star exhibit, but an arresting sight is the room packed with the tombs of 16 Mevlevi sheiks.

From Atatürk Meydanı, Asma Alti Sokagi leads past a couple of old Turkish *hans* (inns) with picturesque courtyards and verandahs: the **Kumarcılar Hanı** (open Mon–Fri) and **Büyük Han** (open Mon and Wed–Thur 8am–8pm, Tue and Fri 8am–midnight, Sat 8am–3pm; free). Built by the Turks in the 18th century as hospices for visiting foreigners, they are rare survivors of their kind on the island.

To the east are the minarets and lofty Gothic arches of the **Selimiye Mosque** (open daily dawn–dusk; donation expected), formerly the great Cathedral of the Holy Wisdom, begun in 1209 and completed in the 14th century. The Lusignans were crowned kings of Cyprus and Christians worshipped here until the Turks turned it into a mosque after the 1570 conquest.

Next door is the **Bedesten**, or old covered market, which dates from the 12th to the 14th century, when it was built as the church of St Nicholas-of-the-English. The Turks converted it into a covered market – today disused. You can still admire the Gothic doors and religious sculptures, the barrel-shaped roof and the dome. It now holds a Museum of Medieval Tombstones, but opening times are erratic. Behind the mosque is the **Sultan's Library** (open daily, summer 9am–2pm, winter 9am–1pm and 2–4.45pm; admission fee) housing important books in Turkish, Arabic and Persian.

## The Mountain Castles

North of Nicosia the terrain rises to the Pentadaktylos (Beşparmak) Mountains, which Lawrence Durrell, who lived here from 1953 to 1956, described in *Bitter Lemons* as 'the *par excellence* Gothic range for it is studded with crusader

### Visiting the North

There are currently five crossing-points along the buffer zone that separates North and South. The oldest and of most interest to visitors on foot is at the UN checkpoint on the Green Line in Nicosia, which lies close to the Pafos Gate, at the old Ledra Palace Hotel. Border crossings for vehicles are at Agios Dometios (Metehan) in the western suburbs of Nicosia; at Pergamos (Beyarmudu) and Agios Nikolaos (Akyar), both of which lie within the Dhekelia British Sovereign Base Area, close to Famagusta (Gazimağusa); and at Astromeritis-Kato Zodeia (As Boştancı), west of Nicosia and close to Morfou (Güzelyurt). At the time of writing, further crossing-points were being negotiated.

The procedure for crossing from the South to the North is straightforward, though since the border's opening in 2003 there have been crowds of visitors, and frequent queues. Officially the border opens at 8am and closes for returning visitors at midnight. The police may ask to see your passport.

There is currently no limit on the number of times you may cross. EU citizens have the right of unrestricted movement throughout Cyprus; there may be restrictions for non-EU citizens, though these may not be enforced.

castles pitched on the dizzy spines of the mountains, commanding the roads which run over the saddles between'. The range's most striking peak is the stark silhouette of Pentadaktylos (Five Fingers).

The castles now lie in noble ruin, victims not of enemy bombardment but of demolition by the Venetians. Most spectacular is **Agios Ilarion Castle** (open daily, summer 9am–5pm, winter 9am–1pm and 2–4.45pm; admission fee), which climbs along knife-edge ridges in three tiers of battlements and towers, reaching an altitude of 670m (2,200ft) under twin peaks, with steps leading up and down in all directions.

The castle was built in the 10th century around an earlier church and monastery honouring the hermit saint Ilarion, who fled here when the Arabs advanced on Syria. The original Byzantine structure was fortified and extended by the Lusignans as a summer residence. The views here down to

Pentadaktylos (Five Finger) Mountain

Keryneia harbour are superb and, on a clear day, see the mountains of southern Turkey some 100km (60 miles) away.

Another dramatic castle worth seeing is **Voufaventon**, to the east. This is the island's highest fortress, at 954m (3,130ft), and is often shrouded in mist.

Fisherman at Keryneia

## Keryneia (Girne)

Offering the most beautiful sheltered harbour in Cyprus and a grand old castle, the charming town of **Keryneia** – Girne in Turkish – is the most strikingly situated of the island's towns. The venerable buildings that line the harbour have almost all been converted into bars or restaurants, but compared with the resorts on the south coast, Keryneia is still relaxed and understated.

Overlooking the harbour is the massive bulk of **Keryneia Castle** (open daily, summer 9am–7pm, winter 9am–1pm and 2–4.45pm; admission fee), which dates mostly from the 15th century. Today, its walls enclose a Byzantine chapel, royal apartments and various historical displays, including the **Kyrenia ship**, one of the oldest vessels ever recovered from the sea (and featured on three of the Cypriot euro coins). This Greek trading ship sank near Cyprus around 300BC and was discovered in 1965 by a sponge diver. The surviving hull has been painstakingly preserved and is shown with part of its cargo.

In the foothills behind Keryneia is the superbly sited Gothic abbey of **Belapais** (Beylerbeyi; open daily summer

Belapais Abbey

9am–7pm, winter 9am–1pm and 2–4.45pm; admission fee). Facing the sea, it stands on a 30-m (100-ft) escarpment, its buildings enclosing cypresses, palms and orange trees. The abbey was built by the Lusignans and took on its present form in the 13th century. The elegant cloister is adorned with finely carved figures, while the splendid vaulted refectory has six bays and a fine rose window.

## West of Keryneia

You can follow the line of the Pentadaktylos range west to their end, and continue on through the Lebanese Maronite village of **Kormakitis** (Koruçam) to the scenic tip of **Cape Kormakitis**. Southward around the curve of Morfou Bay is the old bishop's seat of **Morfou** (Güzelyurt) and its venerable **Agios Mamas Monastery** (open daily, summer 9am–7pm, winter 9am–1pm and 2–4.45pm; admission fee).

On the narrow strip of Northern Cyprus squeezed between the buffer zone and the sea lie the remains of the ancient (6th-century BC) Graeco-Roman town of **Soloi** (Soli; open daily, summer 9am–7pm, winter 9am–1pm and 2–4.45pm; admission fee) and those of the Persian-era (5th-century BC) palace at **Vouni** (Vuni; open daily, summer 10am–5pm, winter 9am–1pm and 2–4.45pm; admission fee).

## The Karpasia Peninsula

If you have time – don't attempt this if you are on a day trip from South Nicosia – you can take a long, exhilarating drive east of Keryneia, all the way into the long 'panhandle' of the Karpasia (Karpaz) Peninsula. Close to the peninsula's spray-tossed tip are the whitewashed walls of the historic **Apostolos Andreas Monastery** (open daily summer 9am–7pm, winter 9am–1pm and 2–4.45pm; admission fee). Since 2003, pilgrims have been able to pray for miracles at the icon of St Andrew in the monastery's 18th-century church.

## Famagusta (Gazimağusa)

The east coast port of **Famagusta** (Ammochostos/Gazimağusa) was a mere village when Christian refugees arrived from Palestine in 1291. Soon it developed into a boom town of extravagant merchants and notorious courtesans, becoming one of the wealthiest cities in the world. It all ended in 1374 when the Genoese took the port amid much bloodshed. Worse was to come in 1571, with the Turkish invasion and the most famous siege in the island's history *(see page 17)*.

Famagusta rose again in the 20th century to become the most important port in Cyprus and a major tourist centre. But once again, in 1974, a Turkish invasion was to leave the city a mere shadow of its former self. Since the departure of the Greek Cypriots, **Varosha**, the pre-1974 beach resort area, is eerily deserted and off-limits, its hotels, cafés and apartments crumbling and decrepit. Yet

Famagusta's citadel, the Tower of Othello

the Venetian fortifications and old town where Turkish Cypriots have always traditionally lived are still of great interest.

Beside the harbour stands the Citadel, better known as the **Tower of Othello** (open daily, summer 9am–7pm, winter 9am–1pm and 2–4.45pm; admission fee), which is associated with a 16th-century governor of Cyprus, Christoforo Moro, sometimes cited as the model for Shakespeare's tormented Moor. Most formidable of the Venetian fortifications is the **Martinengo Bastion** in the northwest corner of the old town. Its walls, 4–6m (13–19ft) thick, provided stubborn resistance to the Turks during the siege of 1570–1.

Converted from a cathedral, Lala Mustafa Paşa Mosque

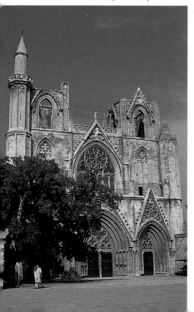

The town's many churches were founded by the Lusignans. The finest was St Nicholas' Cathedral, where the Lusignan kings were crowned as 'kings' of Jerusalem. It was converted into the **Lala Mustafa Paşa Mosque** (open daily dawn–dusk), named after the commander of the Turkish invasion. The handsome structure was completed in 1326 with a majestic western façade worthy of any great European cathedral. Although the Turks stripped the interior of any human representation in sculpture or fresco – and there was damage from an earthquake in 1735 – it can still be admired for its fine Gothic features.

## Salamis

Overlooking the sea just 8km (5 miles) north of Famagusta, the ancient city of **Salamis** rivals Kourion *(see page 53)* as the island's finest archaeological site. It may lack Kourion's dramatic clifftop setting, but makes up for it with a splendid beach right beside the ruins (open daily, summer 9am–7pm, winter 9am–1pm and 2–4.45pm; admission fee).

For 2,000 years, Salamis rivalled Pafos as the leading city in Cyprus and was a haven for Greek artists and intellectuals exiled from Athens. As Constantia, it became the capital of early-Christian Cyprus in AD350, subsequently suffering from earthquake destruction and disappearing completely after the Arab invasion of 647.

Visible ruins today date from the Hellenistic, Roman and Byzantine periods. The **Roman theatre** probably succeeded an earlier Greek structure and its 50-row auditorium – which is the largest in Cyprus – seated 15,000. Also impressive is the spacious **gymnasium**. The graceful Corinthian columns were brought here from the theatre and re-erected by the Byzantines. In the adjoining **public baths**, you can distinguish the *frigidarium, tepidarium* and *caldarium*. The water was channelled from Kythrea, 40km (25 miles) away, via a Roman aqueduct, parts of which are still standing.

Just west of Salamis is the **Mausoleum of St Barnabas** (open daily, summer 9am–7pm, winter 9am–1pm and 2–4.45pm; admission fee), who accompanied Paul on his mission to Cyprus in AD45. (He was martyred in Salamis at the hands of Jews he was trying to convert.) The rock-cut burial chamber is now empty, but its discovery in AD478 helped the Church of Cyprus achieve autonomy within the Orthodox faith, and led to the building of the monastery nearby. The present drum-domed church was built in 1756 with elements from an earlier 15th-century church and columns and capitals from Salamis. It is now a museum of Byzantine icons.

# WHAT TO DO

Cyprus offers plenty to do beyond sightseeing. Sporting activities benefit from a great climate and clear coastal waters, while entertainment ranges from some of the Mediterranean's hottest nightclubs in Agia Napa to more sedate folklore shows at local festivals, and even a play or concert in the grand setting of an ancient open-air amphitheatre.

## SPORTING PURSUITS

The beaches may not all have the best sands, but they do have crystal-clear, unpolluted seas. Hikers can find solitude and marvellous scenery in the unspoilt Troodos and Pentadaktylos mountains, and on the rugged Akamas Peninsula and the gentler Karpasia Peninsula.

### Watersports

Scuba divers and snorkellers are major beneficiaries of Cyprus' limpid seas. In water temperatures ranging from 16°C (60°F) to 27°C (80°F), you can explore submerged cliffs, valleys and caves, and may get close-up views of sea anemones and sponges, exotic coloured fish and crustaceans (although marine life is not abundant in the nutrient-poor eastern Mediterranean). You can also dive on several wrecks, including the car ferry *Zenobia*, which sank off Larnaka in 1980. You will find qualified diving centres with equipment for hire and instruction at Pafos, Coral Bay, Lakki, Larnaka, Limassol, Agia Napa and Protaras in the South, and at Keryneia (Girne) in the North.

Windsurfing and water-skiing are widely available, with equipment for hire at public and hotel beaches. Other

Parasailing off the beach at Agia Napa

Clear water allows for great snorkelling

activities such as jet-skiing and parasailing are available at the main resorts. Serious sailors can hire craft from the harbours at Agia Napa, Pafos, Lakki, Larnaka, Limassol and Keryneia.

## Golf
Golf is not a game much associated with Cyprus, but four excellent courses are well worth seeking out: **Secret Valley**, tucked away in a lovely hidden location not far from Aphrodite's Birthplace; **Aphrodite Hills** close by; **Tsada**, northeast of Pafos; and **Vikla**, near Limassol. All are 18-hole courses with the usual facilities. The North has a nine-hole course, **Cengiz Topel**, at Pentageia (Yeşilyurt).

## Walking and Hiking
The Troodos Mountains, Pentadaktylos Mountains and Akamas Peninsula are ideal for hiking, though most people will

find it too strenuous, or just plain uncomfortable, in summer. If you want to go it alone, the Cyprus Tourism Organisation has maps and information on local itineraries *(see pages 126–8)*. Visit the Pafos or Polis offices for the Akamas Peninsula, the Pano Platres office for the Troodos Mountains (and the Keryneia, Girne) tourist office for the Pentadaktylos, or ask at any CTO office for the excellent *Nature Trails* brochure, which maps out walks all over the south of the island. Adjacent to the Baths of Aphrodite car park, there's a CTO tourist pavilion that has details of walking trails; it is from here that paths lead off into the Akamas.

For organised trekking tours of the Akamas, try the well-respected Exalt Travel (tel: 2531 5154). Their adventurous programme takes in dry river beds, lunar landscapes of chalk plateau, refreshing waterfalls and the spectacular Avakas Gorge. You don't need to be experienced, as long as you are reasonably healthy and have a decent pair of walking shoes.

Experienced hikers in search of adventure in the Troodos may enjoy the nature trails that go from the forestry station

## On Two Wheels

Fancy a spot of mountain-biking? Cyprus has the mountains, and you can hire bikes in all the main resorts. There's little to stop you – except the fact that the mountains are dauntingly high and steep, it's going to be hot up there and the steed you're riding will probably look as if it went through Cyprus with Richard the Lionheart.

If you're sure you can hack it, there's plenty of testing terrain in the Troodos and Pentadaktylos Mountains, on the Akamas Peninsula, around Cape Gkreko and in the wilds of Tillyria, Pitsyllia and Karpasia. Take plenty of water and don't overdo it in summer. Anyone of a less rugged disposition can content themselves with a relaxing cycle along the many quiet, smooth and mostly flat farm roads close to the sea.

## Winter sports

Sporting activities are not limited to the summer on the island. In winter, lifts provide access to four ski runs on Mt Olympos, and cross-country skiing is possible. Depending on snow conditions (which are usually poor), the ski season runs from January to late March.

of **Stavros tis Psokas**, north-west of Kykkos. There's a hostel here that you need to reserve in advance (tel: 2699 9144). Less intimidating are the Atalante and Artemis trails (12km/8 miles and 7km/4 miles respectively) around Mt Olympos *(see page 60)* just below the summit. An easy but rewarding trek will lead you to the Kalidonia Falls *(see page 59)*.

## Extreme Sports

You can augment the hazards of partying in Agia Napa with bungee-jumping at nearby Nissi Beach: the drop is 60m (200ft). Then there is the Slingshot, also in Agia Napa, claimed to be the highest and fastest ride in the world. Riders are propelled to a height of 100m (300ft) in a breathtaking 1.3 seconds.

# SHOPPING

The quality of most tourist shops in Cyprus is low, tending towards cheap, imported tat. Instead you should head for the nearest **Cyprus Handicraft Service** (CHS) shop, showcasing the best of the island's artisans. Compared with elsewhere, goods here are expensive, but they are handmade and have the CHS label to guarantee it. You will find CHS shops at – **Pafos**: 64 Leoforos Apostolou Pavlou; **Limassol**: 25 Odos Themidou; **South Nicosia**: CHS workshop, 186 Leoforos Athalassis; **Larnaka**: 6 Odos Kosma Lysioti. You can also find the works of talented craftspeople in various fields in their own shops and in outlets that stock quality products.

## Best Buys

**Basketry.** The choice ranges from small baskets in decorative shapes and colours to large articles in rush or cane.

**Brass.** Look for candlesticks, ashtrays, small boxes, religious ornaments and trays.

**Ceramics.** Most ceramics are crude and garish. Seek out artisans who look back to antiquity for inspiration, creating charming animal figurines, little vessels and terracotta statuettes. The functional wares from Kornos and Foini include attractive hand-made wine and oil jars.

**Copperware.** After 3,000 years, the copper industry remains a source of Cypriot pride. There are all manner of hand-crafted wares, including pots, saucepans and bowls.

Colourful ceramic souvenirs

**Embroidery.** The island's most important cottage industry items are fine linen tablecloths, doilies, runners and handkerchiefs, stitched with the intricate geometric patterns of *lefkaritika* from Lefkara, and the more colourful *pafitika* from Pafos.

**Food and Wine.** A speciality of Geroskipou, near Pafos, 'Cypriot Delight' is sold all over the island. Never call it Turkish Delight in the South; use its Greek name, *loukoúmi*. You may also want to take home olives or sealed packets of *halloúmi* cheese. Of the many wines and liqueurs produced in Cyprus,

Terracotta urns for sale

the most popular gift is the sweet red dessert wine Commandaria.

**Icons.** Pieces available range from the exquisite works produced by nuns and monks, such as Brother Kallinikos *(see page 45)*, to the cheaper items on sale in most gift shops.

**Jewellery.** You can find good quality silver and gold, the latter is almost always 18-carat, but in the resorts the quality can be poor. Good jewellers will provide a certificate of authenticity.

**Leather Goods.** Manufactured locally, shoes and sandals are reasonably priced in Cyprus.

## ENTERTAINMENT

Most resorts have a tourist-office brochure or a privately produced publication listing what's on. Another good resource is the What's On sections of the *Cyprus Mail* and *Cyprus Weekly* in the South, and of *Cyprus Today* in the North.

### Folklore Shows

Most hotels offer weekly folklore shows with costumed performers singing and dancing to traditional Greek tunes. Visitors are encouraged to get up and dance along. Many tavernas also have Greek Cypriot and Greek dancing on a regular basis.

One local speciality is the glass-balancing routine. A dancer will have an empty glass placed upside down on his head and will dance a few steps to show his balancing agility. It may not be terribly impressive with just one glass, but by the time his colleagues have balanced a 30-glass tower, the crowd is open-mouthed. Another routine involves placing a glass half-full of water into an old-fashioned wooden sieve. The sieve is at first gently swung from side to side, then furiously rotated while the dancer spins like a whirling dervish. The glass and liquid remain in place, and the audience stays dry.

In Northern Cyprus, you may find (and be invited to engage in) belly dancing, and can enjoy Turkish music from enthusiastic if not always terribly talented local combos.

## Historic Venues

The most memorable and distinctive evening's entertainment on offer is a night at the ancient theatre. The **Pafos Odeon** stages plays (in English), and the magnificently situated theatre at **Kourion** is a wonderful place to catch a Shakespeare play or classical drama, or to hear some jazz. If you are staying in Limassol, or even Pafos, it's well worth the effort to get there.

### Nightlife and Agia Napa

Agia Napa aside, nightlife in Cyprus is fairly low key, usually comprising an evening at a restaurant or taverna, followed by a drink in a bar. Some resorts have karaoke bars, live music and nightclubs.

In recent years Agia Napa (see page 46) has become one of the Mediterranean's major party destinations for young holidaymakers. It has a number of clubbing options, from '80s-revival nights to the latest in hardcore sounds. In July and August the crowd is very much 18–30 and can get a bit rowdy at times. However, the authorities operate a 'zero tolerance' policy towards drugs and raucous behaviour, which, for many, has spelled the end of the party. Outside the high season, you will find older, more discerning tastes being catered for. The popular clubs change from season to season, so ask around. And don't go out too early – the real action doesn't start until around 1am.

Dancing in Agia Napa

Hire a cushion, or take along something soft to sit on. Out of high season, you might need a sweater, too. Another pleasant historic outdoor venue is the castle at **Larnaka**, with performances of dance and theatre during the Larnaka Festival in July.

## CHILDREN

With clean beaches and endless sunshine, Cyprus is great for kids (but be sure to protect them from the fierce Mediterranean sun). Cypriots, like most southern Europeans, love children and, safety considerations aside, there are few, if any, restrictions on where they can go.

If you are bored with the beach, but not with the water, there are four water parks to experience. **WaterWorld**, just outside Agia Napa at Agia Thekla, claims to be the biggest water theme park in Europe. It has over 20 rides, ranging from high-speed thrill chutes to the Lazy River. Greek columns, statues and fountains provide the theme. There are three other water parks: **Wet 'n' Wild**, just east of Limassol, is larger and wilder than **Watermania** on the western side of Limassol at Fassouri. The **Paphos Aphrodite Waterpark** between Pafos and Geroskipou also has its superlatives, including a long rafting ride and a plunging descent called the Kamikazi.

The biggest and best amusement park is **La Luna Fun Fair** in Agia Napa. Kids will also enjoy the **glass-bottomed boat rides** from virtually all resorts, and a 30-seat miniature **Yellow Submarine** tour of the underwater world from Agia Napa.

# Festivals and Holy Days

**January** *Ta Fota*. On Epiphany Day (6 January), bishops bless the waters in all the seaside towns, throwing Limassol's Holy Crosses into the sea. Youngsters dive for them.

**February/March** *Carnival*. Limassol's 10-day long celebration features fancy-dress balls and a spate of parades. It's not Rio, but it's fun.

**March/April** *Good Friday*. Solemn Orthodox Masses take place all over Cyprus, with a procession of the Holy Sepulchre along main thoroughfares. *Easter*. A midnight service takes place on the Saturday before Easter, when people light their candles from the priest's, moving around the church and chanting the litany. Once the service is over, spectacular firework displays begin. On Easter Sunday, high Masses celebrate the resurrection of Christ.

**May/June** *Kataklysmos*. The Festival of the Flood coincides with Pentecost, and this two-day holiday harks back to ancient times, when Cypriots convened at temples to worship and sacrifice to Adonis and Aphrodite. Today, there are excursions to the beach, parties, games, colourful parades and competitions – especially in Pafos.

*Nicosia Arts Festival*. This two-week event in June features everything from art exhibits and folk dancing to avant-garde ballet and rock concerts.

*Ancient Greek Drama Festival*. This festival of classical Greek theatre takes place between June and August. Plays are performed on warm summer evenings against the spectacular backdrops of the island's ancient open-air amphitheatres, such as the ones at Pafos and Kourion.

**July** *Larnaka Festival*. During this historically oriented festival, dance and theatre performances are staged at the castle in Larnaka.

**August** *Assumption of the Virgin*. On 15 August, the faithful gather at the leading monasteries and churches. This is the most important day in the Greek religious festival calendar. Beware – the crowds are massive.

**September** *Limassol* Wine Festival. A fortnight of wine-tastings, dancing and folklore shows. (Note that this event may begin in late August.)

*Agia Napa Festival*. This well-established festival of folklore, music, dance and theatre attracts large crowds.

# EATING OUT

The food of Cyprus will be familiar to anyone who has visited Greece (or, in the case of Northern Cyprus, Turkey). Basically, it comprises grilled meats and fish, salads and a small selection of speciality casseroles. Strangely, vegetables, though grown in abundance on the island, rarely find their way on to restaurant tables.

At its best, Cypriot cooking is simple, hearty and healthy. Unfortunately, with mass tourism has come that bland hybrid called 'international cuisine', and worse still, mass catering has impacted badly on the local food. Bright-pink factory-produced *taramasalata* and imitation crab sticks are now passed off in some places as part of a traditional fish *meze (see page 97).*

### New creations

For the latest thing, look for sophisticated restaurants serving 'New Cypriot Cuisine', reinterpreting the old standards in new and intriguing ways, and adding touches of international fusion.

## Where to Eat

Many tourist-orientated restaurants now simply cook to a price, and if you are at all serious about your food, you should choose very carefully where you eat. Unlike in Greece, where you're encouraged to go into the kitchen to point out what you'd like to eat, Cypriot restaurants usually expect you to order from the menu (which is nearly always translated into English). Some traditional tavernas have no menu, just a set meal, and you pay a fixed price for whatever is being served that night. Trust them and enjoy your meal. Cypriots are known for their generosity, and restaurateurs are no exception. In a good local restaurant, fresh fruit,

Greek coffee, perhaps even the local wine, may well be on the house. You should return the gesture with a generous tip.

Note that the terms *taverna* and restaurant are often used loosely in Cyprus, though the former implies an informal, even rustic traditional eating and drinking establishment.

## Fast Food and Starters

Cypriot fast food generally means a *pita* bread stuffed with *sheftalia* (a kind of sausage) or *souvláki*, a kebab of grilled cubes of fresh lamb or goat, plus salad, and a yogurt dressing. The ingredients will be fresh and the *sheftalia* homemade, with local herbs. You'll get these snacks at small takeaways or cafés. They are the cheapest and arguably one of the healthiest ways of filling up.

Common to nearly all restaurants serving Cypriot-style food are four dips: *taramasalata*, a pink fish-roe paste made

A classic Greek salad

with olive oil and lemon juice, and thickened with mashed potato or softened bread; *talatoura*, a Cypriot variant of the Greek *tzatziki* (yoghurt with cucumber, crushed garlic and fresh mint); *tahini*, a sesame-seed paste with garlic; and *hummus*, puréed chick-peas, olive oil and spices. To accompany these dips, you'll be served either fresh Cypriot sesame-seed bread *(koulouri)* or *pita* bread.

*Koupépia*, is another well-known starter, also known as *dolmádes* or *dolmadaki* – vine leaves stuffed with rice and lamb, flavoured with mint. Another Greek staple, stuffed vegetables, is not common in Cyprus. Two more permanent items on the starter section of a menu are *loúnza*, a thinly sliced fillet of smoked pork, and *halloúmi*, a Cypriot ewe's-milk cheese. Both of these may be served hot (chargrilled or fried) or cold, and are often offered as a combination. Much less commonly found on restaurant menus is *loukanika*, a Cypriot smoked sausage.

Dining alfresco

Local soups are not common on menus (apart from the ubiquitous vegetable soup, which is usually made from leftovers). But if you do get the chance, try *avgolemono*, a lemon-flavoured chicken broth thickened with egg and served with rice. Another rarity to look out for is *kypriakes ravioles*, Cypriot ravioli stuffed with *halloúmi*, eggs and mint.

## Meat Dishes and Vegetables

Almost without exception, every restaurant that serves Greek-Cypriot food in the tourist resorts has a section on its menu entitled Cypriot Specialities. Invariably, it includes the following dishes: *moussaka*, a layered dish of minced meat, aubergine and potatoes, with a bechamel sauce and spices; *afelia*, a tender pork stew made with red wine, cumin and coriander seeds; *kléftiko*, oven-roasted lamb with mint, the traditional Sunday lunch for the locals; *stifádo*, a catch-all term for a stew of tomatoes, herbs, olive oil and vinegar that usually features beef; *keftédes*, meat balls flavoured with herbs, usually coriander and cumin. Less common but well worth trying is *távas*, lamb or pork cooked in a clay pot with vegetables and spices. A variety of plain grilled steaks and chops also feature on all menus.

Vegetable dishes and accompaniments are scarce. In the tourist quarters, everything is served with French fries and either Greek or 'Village-style' salad, which are one and the same and contain lettuce or cabbage, cucumber, tomatoes, possibly olives and always a thick slice or two of *feta* cheese.

In more authentic restaurants, you should be able to get *louvia* (black-eyed beans) or *fasólia* (which may also be black-eyed beans or large white beans, usually served cold

### Meze

Meze, strictly speaking, are appetisers, though the meze which many restaurants in Cyprus offer indicates a full meal (in fact a meal and a half!). A typical Cypriot meze consists of some 20-plus small dishes with a mixture of appetisers and small portions of main courses. It is an excellent crash course in Cypriot food and is usually good value, though invariably it must be ordered by a minimum of two people. The choice is usually meat meze or fish meze. Don't be afraid to ask what's in it. Keep in mind that although the portions are small, they do add up.

in a tomato and onion sauce), green beans or peas, tomatoes, courgettes and aubergine. Look out too for *kolokássia*, made from taro root, a relative of the yam.

## Fish and Shellfish

As offshore catches get smaller and smaller, the choice of seafood becomes more limited and prices increase accordingly. Octopus *(chtapodi)* is often served in a red wine sauce. Prawns *(garídes)*, battered squid *(kalamari)* and spiny lobster are common menu items, but may be frozen, not fresh. This should be indicated on the menu but, if in doubt, ask.

Fresh fish that is generally available is swordfish *(xifías)*, red mullet *(barboúnia)*, red snapper *(sinagrida)*, gilt-head bream *(tsipoúra)* and sometimes whitebait *(marídes)*. Fish is usually simply barbecued. The speciality of the Troodos Mountains is farmed trout – smoked, sautéed or *au bleu* (poached with clarified butter).

## Desserts and Sweets

Dessert usually means ice cream or fruit. Go for the latter. Depending on the season, you'll be able to try the island's outstanding honeydew and cantaloupe melons, watermelon, cherries, peaches, figs, apricots, oranges, bananas, tangerines, plums, grapes, pomegranates and more.

Cypriot sweets are rarely offered as dessert after a meal, but are sold separately in cafés or at specially set-up stalls. They are often very sweet. Honey and nuts are used in both *baklava*, a layered, strudel-like pastry, and *kataïfi*, a pastry that resembles shredded wheat. Another mouthwatering Cypriot speciality is *loukoumades*, a kind of sweet deep-fried doughnut dipped in syrup.

### Waiting tables

When waiters approach your table they will usually say *Oristeh* – How can I help you/What would you like?

## Coffee

Unless you specify Greek coffee, you will probably be served Nescafé – but not necessarily the brand itself, as this is the generic Greek term for instant coffee. In a DIY fashion, you are provided hot water with a sachet of instant powder. However, more places now offer filter coffee or cappuccino.

If you would prefer to try the local stuff, order *kafé elleniko* (Greek coffee), or simply *kahve* in the North. You will have to specify sweet *(gliko)*, medium-sweet *(metrio)*, or without sugar *(sketo)*. Greek coffee is taken black with a glass of

Oranges ready for picking

water. Try not to disturb or drink the thick grounds at the bottom of the cup.

## Wines

Cypriot wines have been known and enjoyed since ancient times. Foremost among them is the sweet red Commandaria, originally produced for the Knights of St John at Kolossi. Celebrated as an apéritif or dessert wine, it is similar to Madeira and worth trying even if you don't normally like sweet wines. Sweet and dry wines of the sherry type are another speciality.

By northern European standards, the quality of Cypriot table wines is low, and a few are virtually undrinkable. It is always worth paying a little more and ordering a branded bottle; the majority are quite palatable, and a few are excellent. In a good restaurant the waiter will help you choose. Bella Pais, a rather bubbly white, makes a good apéritif or dessert wine. Duc de Nicosie is the closest a Cyprus wine comes to Champagne, and is produced using the traditional method.

## Other Alcoholic Drinks

As an after-dinner drink, you may be offered a *zivania*, the local fire water. Distilled from the grape residue, it is similar to Greek *raki*. The other famous Greek drink enjoyed in Cyprus – though more by tourists than by the Cypriots – is *ouzo*, a clear aniseed-flavoured spirit that turns milky with the addition of water. (Confusingly, it is also called *raki* by the Turkish).

If you are going to drink Cypriot brandy straight, go for one of the better-known, more expensive brands, to avoid

**Cypriot wines have been appreciated since antiquity**

throat burn. A much more common use for local brandy is as the base for a brandy sour, the traditional island sundowner.

The local lagers (always referred to as beer), Keo and Leon are very good. Carlsberg is also brewed on the island.

## To Help You Order...

| | |
|---|---|
| Could we have a table? | **Tha boroúsame na échoume éna trapézi?** |
| I'd like a/an/some ... | **Tha íthela ...** |

| | | | |
|---|---|---|---|
| beer | **mía bíra** | milk | **gála** |
| bread | **psomí** | mineral water | **metallikó neró** |
| coffee | **éna kafé** | napkin | **petséta** |
| cutlery | **macheropírouna** | potatoes | **patátes** |
| dessert | **éna glikó** | rice | **rízi** |
| fish | **psári** | salad | **mía saláta** |
| fruit | **froúta** | soup | **mía soúpa** |
| glass | **éna potíri** | sugar | **záchari** |
| honey | **méli** | tea | **éna tsäï** |
| ice cream | **éna pagotó** | wine | **krasí** |
| meat | **kréas** | | |

## ...and Read The Menu

| | | | |
|---|---|---|---|
| **afélia** | pork stew | **loúnza** | smoked pork |
| **barboúnia** | red mullet | **marídes** | whitebait |
| **fasólia** | beans | **souvláki** | kebab |
| **garídes** | prawns | **stifádo** | stew (usually beef) with tomatoes |
| **halloúmi** | ewe's milk cheese | | |
| **keftédes** | meatballs | **távas** | casserole in clay pot (usually lamb or pork) |
| **kléftiko** | roast lamb | | |
| **kolokássia** | taro root ('Cypriot spinach') | | |
| | | **tsipoúra** | gilthead bream |
| **koupépia** | stuffed vine leaves | **xifías** | swordfish |

# HANDY TRAVEL TIPS

An A–Z Summary of Practical Information

# A

**ACCOMMODATION** *(see also CAMPING, YOUTH HOSTELS, and HOTELS AND RESTAURANTS)*

In the high season (mid-June to October), try to book well in advance. The Cyprus Tourism Organisation *(see pages 126–8)* produces a brochure listing virtually all hotels and many other types of accomodation. If you arrive without a booking, contact the CTO at the airport or in Nicosia, Larnaka, Limassol, Pafos, Agia Napa, Polis or Pano Platres for advice.

**Hotels.** Cyprus has hotels in all categories, from five-star luxury havens and comfortable guest-houses to pleasant apartment-hotels (classified A, B, C and Tourist Apartments). In general, standards are high and prices are reasonable compared with other resorts and islands. All hotels offer discounts during the low season, which for seaside resorts is from 16 November to 15 March, and for hill resorts from 1 October to 30 June – both excluding the Christmas/New Year and Easter holiday periods.

**Villas.** Self-contained villas may be rented through local agencies, or you can inquire at the CTO. Unlike on the small Greek islands, accommodation in unregistered private houses is not available.

**Agrotourism.** Thanks to an initiative by the CTO, some traditional houses in the countryside have been renovated and are now rented out as holiday homes. For details, ask the CTO for a brochure or contact the Cyprus Agrotourism Company, 19 Leoforos Lemesou, PO Box 24535, 1390 Nicosia, Cyprus; tel: 2234 0071; <www.agrotourism.com.cy>.

| | |
|---|---|
| I'd like a single/double room | Tha íthela éna monó/dipló domátio |
| with bath/shower | me bánio/dous |
| What's the rate per night? | Piá íne i timí giá mía níkta? |

## AIRPORTS

**Larnaka International Airport** (tel: 778833), the principal air gateway to Cyprus, lies 5km (3 miles) from Larnaka town and 50km (30 miles) from Nicosia. Taxis are available from the airport to both cities, while shared taxis and minibuses, scheduled frequently during the day, provide inexpensive transport for three or more passengers sharing the cost. A few local buses operate daily to Larnaka.

A replacement for Nicosia airport, which in 1974 was designated United Nations territory and is no longer in use, Larnaka airport has been modernised and expanded to cope with increased demand. It has a duty-free shop, snack bar, restaurant, currency exchange, car-hire agencies, post office and tourist information office. At peak hours in the high season make sure you arrive with plenty of time to spare before your flight departure.

**Pafos International Airport** (tel: 778833), 11km (7 miles) southeast of Pafos on the west coast, handles some scheduled and many charter services, which helps to ease the congestion at Larnaka. And expansion has allowed it to cope better with peak passenger flows. It has a duty-free shop, currency-exchange facilities, car-hire agencies, snack-bar restaurants and a tourist information office.

The airport at **Ercan** (tel: 231 4806) in Northern Cyprus, 14km (9 miles) east of Nicosia, is served by flights from Turkey only. It has been declared by the Republic of Cyprus prohibited port of entry and exit.

| | |
|---|---|
| Porter! Take these bags to the bus/taxi, please. | **Parakaló! Pigénete aftés tis aposkevés sto leoforío/taxi.** |

## ANTIQUITIES

It is illegal to remove antiquities, stones and other remains from any archaeological site, including the seabed. The purchase and export of antiquities is strictly regulated, and export permission must be granted by the Director of the Department of Antiquities, c/o Ministry of Communications and Works, Nicosia.

## B

## BIKE AND MOTORCYCLE HIRE

You can hire bikes and motorcycles in all important towns. To operate a motorcycle or motor scooter, you must be at least 18 years of age and hold a driver's licence (17-year-olds may hire a moped of 49cc). It is illegal not to wear a crash helmet and the police are more likely to enforce this regulation these days. Moped hire is cheap (about €10/C£6 per day), but check your holiday insurance covers you.

Mountain biking, particularly in the Troodos Mountains and Pentadaktylos (Beşparmak) Mountains, and on the Akamas Peninsula, is popular but strenuous, so be sure you are up to the challenge before setting out. Cycling along the coast is far easier. The CTO *(see page 127)* has a brochure, *Cyprus for Cycling*, detailing 19 routes in the South. For more details, call the Cyprus Cycling Federation; tel: 2266 3344; fax: 2266 1150.

## BUDGETING FOR YOUR TRIP

Pricewise, Cyprus is above average as a Mediterranean destination – more expensive than most Greek islands, Turkey and parts of Spain and southern Portugal, but cheaper than much of mainland Europe. In high season, airfares from Britain cost around £200–300 and a good four-star hotel's room rate is around €145 per night. Booking a package, particularly at the last minute, will save you money.

Food and drink is moderate (a three-course meal plus drinks in a simple restaurant usually comes to around €20 per person). Car hire starts from about €40 per day, including Collision Damage Waiver (and by shopping around you can sometimes do better). Public transport and museum fees are inexpensive; private attractions such as waterparks are more expensive.

# C

## CAMPING

Official campsites in the South are licensed by the Cyprus Tourism Organisation. They provide electricity, toilets, showers, a food shop and often a café. There are five official sites: Troodos; Polis; Governor's Beach, near Limassol; Geroskipou, near Pafos; and Feggari/Coral Bay, near Pafos. Ask at the nearest CTO office *(see page 127)* or the local police station for local, unlisted campsites.

| | |
|---|---|
| Is there a campsite nearby? | **Ipárchi éna méros giá kataskínosi/'camping' edó kondá?** |

## CAR HIRE *(see also Driving)*

As many sights in Cyprus are spread out, and beyond the reach of public transport, it is worth hiring a car.

Budget, Thrifty, Hertz, Avis and Eurodollar all have offices in the major cities in the South, and representatives at Larnaka and Pafos airports and at the main resorts. Rates are cheap (from around €30 per day), though you will have to add another €10 or so for Collision Damage Waiver insurance, and perhaps another €2 to cover damage to the tyres or windscreen. For a decent family-sized car, plan on spending up to €50 per day. In summer, air-conditioning is essential. Cypriot firms generally charge less than international firms and some of them provide equally good cars and service. Note that the rate always includes unlimited mileage.

Reserve a car in advance – especially for the high season. To hire a car, you must have a valid national driver's licence (held for at least three years) or an International Driving Permit. Depending on the company, the minimum age is 21 to 25. Drivers under 25 pay an insurance premium. A deposit is usually required, payable by credit card. Check whether driving on unsurfaced roads will invalidate the insurance, and on the position with taking the car into the North.

| | |
|---|---|
| I'd like to hire a car (tomorrow) for one day/a week | **Tha íthela na nikiáso éna aftokínito (ávrio) giá mía iméra/mía evdomáda** |
| Please include full insurance. | **Sas parakaló na simberilávete plíri asfália.** |

## CLIMATE

Cyprus enjoys sunny skies and low humidity almost year-round. On the coast, sea breezes temper the 32°C (90°F) heat of July and August, but in Nicosia you can add on 4 or 5 degrees, and the thermometer often goes above 38°C (100°F).

January and February see snowfalls in the Troodos range – most years enough to allow some skiing. It rains occasionally between October and February, but there's plenty of sun, too, and the sea remains just about warm enough for swimming.

The following are average coastal temperatures:

|        | J  | F  | M  | A  | M  | J  | J  | A  | S  | O  | N  | D  |
|--------|----|----|----|----|----|----|----|----|----|----|----|----|
| max °C | 17 | 17 | 19 | 23 | 26 | 30 | 32 | 33 | 31 | 27 | 22 | 18 |
| °F     | 63 | 63 | 66 | 73 | 79 | 86 | 90 | 91 | 88 | 81 | 72 | 64 |
| min °C | 8  | 8  | 9  | 12 | 16 | 19 | 21 | 21 | 20 | 16 | 12 | 9  |
| °F     | 46 | 46 | 48 | 54 | 61 | 66 | 70 | 70 | 68 | 61 | 54 | 48 |

## CLOTHING

In summer, wear comfortable, loose cotton clothing. July and August nights are very warm, but at other times of the year, they can be cool (so can air-conditioned rooms), so a light sweater is a good idea. In winter (late November to March), you'll need a raincoat or light winter coat, a warm sweater or jacket, and warmer clothes. On the beach, toplessness is widely tolerated; however, nudity in public is unacceptable. Take along a cover-up for the beach-bar – not just for modesty, but because cool sea breezes do blow up. Informality is the general rule, but in the more posh hotels and restaurants, people often dress up in the evening (and may be required to do so). Men will need long trousers to visit Orthodox monasteries and women must wear a long skirt (often provided) and a modest top.

## CRIME AND SAFETY

There is still so little crime on Cyprus that the few robberies which do take place make headlines, but crime rates are rising. The island's only violence generally occurs in drunken brawls in Agia Napa and other busy tourist centres. Cypriots are normally very honest, but your fellow tourists and some migrant workers may not be, so take the usual precautions of locking your hire car and depositing money and jewellery in the hotel safe.

## CUSTOMS AND ENTRY REQUIREMENTS

**Entering the Republic.** Nationals of the EU, Australia, Canada, Japan, New Zealand, Singapore, the US and some other countries can stay in Cyprus for up to three months without a visa. Legal points of entry are the ports of Larnaka, Limassol and Pafos, and the international airports of Larnaka and Pafos.

**Entering the North.** Visitors travelling via Ercan airport or the ports of Famagusta (Gazimağusa), Keryneia (Girne) or Karavostasi (Gemikonağı) in Turkish-controlled Northern Cyprus, and who are citizens of countries that do not require a visa to enter Cyprus, may cross freely in both directions between North and South at the official crossing points. But if they are resident in the North for 90 days or more, they may require a residency permit issued by the authorities in the South to be able to cross without hindrance. Note that the regulations, their implementation, and exceptions and waivers, may change frequently and without notice.

**Customs.** Formalities are minimal, although there are sometimes long waits at passport control. Luggage may be opened for inspection.

Southern Cyprus joined the European Union in 2004, and since then there have been no restrictions on the import by travellers arriving from another EU country of (legal) goods for personal use. Guidelines for what constitutes personal use are about four times the amounts permitted for travellers arriving from non-EU countries in the case of tobacco products, and up to 10 times in the case of alcoholic drinks (amounts may vary per category). Travellers to the Republic from non-EU countries may import the following tax-free: 200 cigarettes or 100 cigarillos or 50 cigars or 250g of tobacco; 1 litre of spirits or 2 litres of fortified wines and 2 litres of other wines; and one bottle of perfume (not exceeding 50g) and toilet water (not exceeding 0.25 litres).

**Currency restrictions.** You may import or export any currency up to the equivalent of €12,500.

| | |
|---|---|
| I've nothing to declare. | **Den écho típota na dilóso.** |
| It's for my personal use. | **Íne giá prosopikí chrísi.** |

# D

## DRIVING

**Road conditions.** Driving conditions are generally good in Cyprus, with well-surfaced, well-marked roads and fast motorways running along the south coast, linking Limassol, Larnaka, Agia Napa and Pafos, and heading inland to Nicosia. Beware of speeding on these roads as there are frequent police patrols. Most of the main roads are paved and in good condition, and even many of the secondary roads are easily negotiated. Short distances on minor roads, typically in the hills, can often be tackled in an ordinary car, but they are often unpaved and pock-marked with potholes in addition to having steep, hairpin turns. You should be alert at all times on these roads. A four-wheel-drive vehicle is best for this kind of driving. There are many rough tracks, which may invalidate your hire-car insurance.

City traffic is fairly orderly. During the rush hour, you can expect to encounter traffic jams in Nicosia, Larnaka, Limassol and Pafos.

**Rules and regulations.** British and Irish motorists will feel at home in Cyprus, where traffic keeps to the left. Seat-belt use is compulsory in the front of cars and, where fitted, in the back, too. Always carry your driving licence and car-hire documents with you.

**Speed limits.** The speed limits are 50kph (30mph) in town and 100kph (60mph) on highways (lower limits may be posted).

**Fuel.** The price of fuel in Cyprus compares with elsewhere in Europe. Diesel fuel is cheaper than petrol, and it is possible to hire diesel cars. Filling stations are plentiful in and around the main towns and resorts, but are scarcer in the mountains. If you're set-

| | |
|---|---|
| Are we on the right road for ...? | **Ímaste sto drómo giá ...?** |
| left/right | **aristerá/dexiá** |
| up/down | **epáno/káto** |
| Full tank, please. | **Na to gemísete me venzíni.** |
| normal/super/lead-free | **aplí/soúper/amólivdos** |
| My car has broken down. | **Épatha mía vlávi.** |
| There's been an accident. | **Égine éna disteíchima.** |
| (international) driving permit | **(diethnís) ádia odigíseos** |
| car registration papers | **ádia kikloforías** |
| collision insurance | **asfália enandíon trítou** |
| Check the oil/tyres/battery. | **Na eléchsete ta ládia/ta lá ticha/ti bataría.** |

ting out on a mountain excursion, make sure the tank is full. Filling stations generally close on Sundays and public holidays, but many have self-service fuel pumps that take cash or credit cards.

**Parking.** This can be a problem in Nicosia, Limassol, Pafos, Agia Napa and Larnaka. Fines are given for illegal parking. Try to find a meter or car park.

**Problems.** Call the hire company first, then try the Cyprus Automobile Association; tel: 2231 3131 (24-hour assistance). In an emergency, call the police, tel: 112 (in the North 155).

**Road signs.** Most road signs, and most other signs imparting general information, are the standard pictographs used throughout Europe, and all the written signs are in both English and Greek (in the North the signs are in Turkish and English):

| | |
|---|---|
| ΑΠΑΓΟΡΕΥΕΤΑΙ Η ΑΝΑΜΟΝΗ | No waiting |
| ΑΠΑΓΟΡΕΥΕΤΑΙ Η ΕΙΣΟΔΟΣ | No entry |
| ΑΠΑΓΟΡΕΥΕΤΑΙ Η ΣΤΑΘΜΕΥΣΙΣ | No parking |
| ΔΙΑΒΑΣΙΣΠΕΖΩΝ | Pedestrian crossing |
| ΕΛΤΤΩΣΑΤΕ ΤΑΧΥΤΗΤΑ | Reduce speed |
| ΕΠΙΚΙΝΔΥΝΗ ΚΑΤΩΦΕΡΕΙΑ | Dangerous incline |
| ΕΡΓΑ ΕΠΙ ΤΗΣ ΟΔΟΥ | Road work in progress |
| ΚΙΝΔΥΝΟΣ | Caution |
| ΜΟΝΟΔΡΟΜΟΣ | One-way traffic |
| ΠΑΡΑΚΑΜΠΤΗΡΙΟΣ | Diversion (detour) |
| ΠΟΡΕΙΑ ΥΠΟΧΡΕΩΤΙ ΚΗ ΔΕΞΙΑ | Keep right |
| ΑΛΤ/ΣΤΟΠ | Stop |

## E

## ELECTRICITY

The standard current is 240 volts, 50 Hz AC; sockets are usually three-pin, as in the UK. Adapters are available in hotels and shops. Most hotels and some apartments have 110-volt outlets for razors.

| | |
|---|---|
| I need an adapter/ battery, please. | **Chriázome éna metaschimatistí/ mia bataría, parakaló.** |

## EMBASSIES AND CONSULATES

**Australia**  High Commission, 4 Odos Annis Komninis, Nicosia; tel: 2275 3001

**Canada**  Consulate, 1 Odos Lampousas, Nicosia; tel: 2277 5508

**Ireland**  Chancery, 7 Odos Aiantas, Nicosia; tel: 2281 8183

**UK**  High Commission, Odos Alexandrou Palli, Nicosia; tel: 2286 1100

**USA**  Embassy, Corner of Odos Metochiou and Odos Ploutarchou, Egkomi, Nicosia; tel: 2239 3939

## EMERGENCIES

**Republic of Cyprus:** Police, ambulance and fire brigade: 112
**Northern Cyprus:** Police: 155; ambulance: 112; fire brigade: 199
**Hospitals:** Nicosia, tel: 2260 3000; Larnaka, tel: 2480 0500;
Limassol, tel: 2580 1100; Pafos, tel: 2680 3145;
Paralimni (also for Agia Napa), tel: 2320 0200;
Polis (also for Lakki), tel: 2682 1800

| | | | |
|---|---|---|---|
| Careful | **Prosochí** | Police | **Astinomía** |
| Help | **Voíthia** | Stop | **Stamatíste** |

# G

## GETTING THERE (see also Airports)

For the great majority of people, air travel is the only practical way of getting to Cyprus. Direct scheduled and charter flights link several British airports to Larnaka and Pafos. The flying time is around 4 hours 30 minutes. There are no non-stop flights from North America, but connecting services operate to Larnaka from major cities including New York, Miami, Los Angeles and San Francisco. Most Australian travellers to Cyprus fly by way of Athens, Istanbul or London, while the most direct route from New Zealand is via Milan and Athens. The usual routing to Larnaka from South Africa involves changing planes in Lusaka or Athens.

## GUIDES AND TOURS

There are various guided coach tours that cover such places as Kykkos Monastery and the Troodos Mountains, Pafos, Nicosia and Kourion.

Some of the most interesting tours on the island are run by a company called Exalt (short for Excursion Alternatives; tel: 2531 5154), who specialise in off-the-beaten track jeep and trekking expeditions, devoted to environmentally-friendly exploration of the Cypriot wilderness. Their principal geographical area of expertise is the Akamas Peninsula and the Pafos Forest region, but they also cover parts of the Troodos Mountains.

Taxi drivers can be hired for half-day or full-day tours. Most drivers speak English, and are willing to negotiate a reasonable fare for tours.

# H

## HEALTH AND MEDICAL CARE (see also EMERGENCIES)

Medical treatment and assistance is offered free of charge to tourists in case of emergency, but to be completely at ease, it is recommended that you take out travel insurance to cover any risk of illness and accident while on holiday.

There are very capable doctors and dentists in the resorts, cities and larger towns, as well as good hospital facilities. Your hotel will advise you of the nearest doctor and most of them speak English. Doctors on call at weekends are listed in local newspapers or can be contacted as follows: Nicosia, tel: 9090 1422; Agia Napa, tel: 9090 1423; Larnaka, tel: 9090 1424; Limassol, tel: 9090 1425; Pafos, tel: 9090 1426.

Stomach upsets should not be a problem, as hotels and restaurants observe high standards of cleanliness. Tap water is safe to drink. The sun can bronze you, but also burn you. Take it in very small doses at first and use sunscreen, particularly if you have delicate skin.

**Pharmacies** (ΦAPMAKEIO – *farmakío*) are recognised by the sign outside – a red cross on a white background *(for opening hours, see page 121)*. Certain pharmacies offer a 24-hour service – see local papers for listings.

Most medicines sold in the UK, US, Canada and Europe are available, but often require a prescription. Pharmacists can generally advise on minor problems such as cuts, sunburn, blisters and gastric disorders.

| Where's the nearest (all-night) pharmacy? | Pou íne to kondinótero (dianikterévon) farmakío? |
| --- | --- |
| I need a doctor/dentist | Chriázome éna giatró/odontogiatró |
| an ambulance | éna asthenofóro |
| a hospital | nosokomío |
| I have... | Écho... |
| a headache | ponokéfalo |
| a fever | piretós |
| an upset stomach | pónos stí kiliá |

## HOLIDAYS

In addition to their own national holidays, Cypriots also celebrate certain Greek or Turkish holidays. Offices close on the following days. Shops remain open on some holidays: ask locally as to which ones.

| | | |
|---|---|---|
| **1 Jan** | *Protochroniá* | New Year's Day |
| **6 Jan** | *ton Theofaníon* | Epiphany |
| **25 Mar** | *Ikostí Pémti Martíou (tou Evangelismoú)* | Greek Independence Day |
| **1 Apr** | *Iméra enárxeos kipriakoú* | Greek Cypriot National Day |
| **1 May** | *Protomagiá* | Labour Day |
| **15 Aug** | *Dekapentávgoustos (tis Panagías)* | Assumption Day |
| **1 Oct** | *Iméra tis anexartisías (tis Kíprou)* | Cyprus Independence Day |
| **28 Oct** | *Ikostí Ogdói Oktovríou ('Ochi')* | 'No' Day, commemorating Greek defiance of Italian invasion of 1940 |
| **24/25 Dec** | *Christoúgenna* | Christmas Eve/Day |
| **26 Dec** | *Défteri Iméra ton Christougénnon* | St Stephen's Day |

**Movable dates:**

| | |
|---|---|
| *Katharí Deftéra* | 1st Day of Lent/Ash Monday (also known as Green Monday) |
| *Megáli Paraskeví* | Good Friday |
| *Deftéra tou Páscha* | Easter Monday |
| *Kataklyzmós* | Pentecost (Festival of the Flood) |

| | |
|---|---|
| Are you open tomorrow? | **Iste aniktí ávrio?** |

# L

## LANGUAGE

English is spoken almost as a dual language in all the resorts, and is understood by many people in Cyprus, both North and South. It

| A | α | a | as in bar |
| B | β | v | |
| Γ | γ | g | as in 'go' (before i- and e-sounds, pronounce like y in 'yes') |
| Δ | δ | d | like th in 'this' |
| E | ε | e | as in 'get' |
| Z | ζ | z | |
| H | η | i | like ee in 'meet' |
| Θ | θ | th | as in 'thin' |
| I | ι | i | like ee in 'meet' |
| K | κ | k | |
| Λ | λ | l | |
| M | μ | m | |
| N | ν | n | |
| Ξ | ξ | x | like ks in 'thanks' |
| O | o | o | as in 'got' |
| Π | π | p | |
| P | ρ | r | |
| Σ | σ, ς | s | as in 'kiss' |
| T | τ | t | |
| Y | υ | i | like ee in 'meet' |
| Φ | φ | f | |
| X | χ | ch | as in Scottish 'loch' |
| Ψ | ψ | ps | as in tipsy |
| O/Ω | ω | o | as in 'got' |
| OY | ου | oo | as in 'soup' |

is only well off the beaten track that a familiarity with Greek (in South Cyprus) or Turkish (in Northern Cyprus) is useful. If you do speak Greek, be aware that Cypriot Greek can be very different from that spoken in Greece. There is a distinctive accent (often incomprehensible to other Greeks), and about 15 percent of the vocabulary is unique to the island.

The table on the left lists the Greek alphabet with their capital and small forms, followed by the letter to which they correspond in English.

If you don't speak Greek and want to learn some, consult the Berlitz *Greek Phrase Book & Dictionary*. It covers practically all the situations you're likely to encounter during your Cyprus travels, featuring 1,200 words and phrases. Here are a few phrases you'll often want to use:

| | |
|---|---|
| hello | yásoo (informal), yásas (formal) |
| good morning | kaliméra |
| good afternoon/evening | kalispéra |
| good night | kaliníkta |
| goodbye | chérete |
| please | parakaló |
| thank you | efcharistó |
| yes | ne |
| no | óchi |
| I don't speak Greek. | Den miló ellmiká. |
| Do you speak English? | Miláte angliká? |
| excuse me | me sinchoríte |
| you're welcome | parakaló |
| where/when/how | pou/póte/pos |
| how long/how far | póso keró/póso makriá |
| yesterday/today/tomorrow | chthes/símera/ávrio |
| day/week/month/year | iméra/evdomáda/mínas/chrónos |

| | |
|---|---|
| left/right | **aristerá/dexiá** |
| up/down | **epáno/káto** |
| good/bad | **kalós/kakós** |
| big/small | **megálos/mikrós** |
| cheap/expensive | **ftinós/akrivós** |
| open/closed | **aniktós/klistós** |
| here/there | **edó/ekí** |
| free (vacant)/occupied | **eléftheri/kratiméni** |
| early/late | **norís/argá** |
| easy/difficult | **éfkolos/dískolos** |
| What does this mean? | **Ti siméni aftó?** |
| I don't understand. | **Den katalavéno.** |
| Please write it down. | **Parakaló grápste to.** |
| Is there an admission charge? | **Prépi na pliróso ísodo?** |
| Waiter, please! | **Garsóni (garçon), parakaló!** |
| I'd like... | **Tha íthela...** |
| How much is that? | **Póso káni aftó?** |
| Have you something less expensive? | **Échete káti ftinótero?** |
| What time is it? | **Ti óra íne?** |
| Just a minute. | **Éna leptó.** |

# M

## MAPS

The Cyprus Tourism Organisation provides a comprehensive island map and town plans of Nicosia, Limassol, Larnaka, Pafos, Agia Napa and Protaras, and their environs, plus the Troodos Mountains, free of charge to visitors.

There are numerous road maps on sale, most of excellent quality. Try to find the most up to date, though even they may not in-

clude all new roads and improvements. Bookshops and newsagents
in all towns and resorts stock them.

| | |
|---|---|
| I'd like a street plan of... | **Tha íthela éna odikó chárti tis...** |
| a road map of this region | **éna chárti aftís tis periochís** |

## MEDIA

**Newspapers and magazines.** There is a good selection of British
and Irish newspapers and major American weekly news magazines
available. Foreign newspapers generally arrive a day after publication. The *Cyprus Mail*, an English-language daily, has current news
coverage and a good What's On section and weekly review magazine. The *Cyprus Weekly* (also in English) carries lively features and
helpful information. Most resorts have some sort of free What's On
magazine that can be picked up at the tourist office, hotels, restaurants, bars and nightspots. In the North there's *Cyprus Today*, a
weekly newspaper in English.

| | |
|---|---|
| Have you any English-language newspapers? | **Échete anglikés efimerídes?** |

**Radio and TV.** The Cyprus Broadcasting Corporation (CyBC) trans-
mits English-language programmes on FM 91.1, 92.4, 94.2 and 96.5
with a bulletin at 10am. News and features are broadcast 1.30–3pm
and 7pm–8pm (depending upon the season) until midnight. The BBC
World Service and Radio BFBS (British Forces Broadcasting Service)
are on the air 24 hours a day. Some hotels have BBC Radio Five Live.

Nearly all hotels with three or more stars offer cable and satellite television channels, including BBC World, CNN and Sky. British
football matches and other popular sporting events can be watched
on television in bars that subscribe to Sky Sports and/or the BBC.

## MONEY *(see also OPENING HOURS)*

**Currency.** From independence until 31 December 2007, currency in the Republic of Cyprus was the Cyprus pound (C£). Then, on 1 January, 2008, the euro was introduced as the national currency, at an exchange rate of €1.72 to the pound. The Cypriot euro coins have been designed with images of the indigenous moufflon wild sheep (1, 2 and 5 cents), the ancient Kyrenia ship (10, 20 and 50 cents), and the prehistoric idol of Pomos (€1 and €2). The euro banknotes are €5, €10, €20, €50, €100, €200 and €500; if experience in other eurozone countries is anything to go by, the €200 and €500 notes will have little everyday use and will rarely be encountered.

In Northern Cyprus, the New Turkish lira (YTL) will remain.

**Currency exchange.** Hotels change money and traveller's cheques, but you will tend to get much better rates at a bank (ΤΡΑΠΕΖΑ, *trápeza*).

**Cash dispensers (ATMs).** The easiest method of obtaining cash is at an automatic cash dispenser. You'll find them in all resorts and major towns. Depending upon your own individual card charges, this might also be the cheapest way of obtaining money.

**Traveller's cheques.** Traveller's cheques are widely accepted, but are best cashed at a bank.

| | |
|---|---|
| I want to change some pounds/dollars. | **Thélo n alláxo merikés líres/ meriká dollária.** |
| Do you accept traveller's cheques? | **Pérnete traveller's cheques?** |
| Can I pay with this credit card? | **Boró na pliróso me aftí ti pistotikí kárta?** |

**Credit cards.** Major credit cards are welcome as payment in most city shops, hotels and many, but by no means all, restaurants, as well as by all the international and local car-hire firms. Take along your passport to use as identification.

**Cash.** Pounds sterling and US dollars may be accepted by shops or restaurants – but you'll probably get a poor exchange rate. You will want to carry euros with you, particularly for dining out. Some of the restaurants listed in this guide take cash only.

○

## OPENING HOURS

**National museums and archaeological sites.** Open all year Monday– Saturday 9am–5pm, Sunday 10am–1pm. Other museums keep similar but usually shorter hours, and may be closed on Saturday afternoon and all day Sunday (see Where to Go chapter for individual museums).

**Banks.** Monday–Friday 8.15am–12.30pm during July and August. At other times of year, Monday–Friday 8.30am–12.30pm, and 3.15– 4.45pm on Monday only. Some banks in tourist centres reopen, for currency exchange only, 4–7pm (summer) and 3–6pm (winter).

**Pharmacies.** Except for those on extra-hours duty, pharmacies are open Monday–Friday 7.30 or 8am–1pm and 3 or 4–7pm (mornings only on Wednesday and Saturday).

**Restaurants.** Lunch is normally served from approximately 12.30–3pm and dinner from around 7–11.30pm; many restaurants of the less formal kind are open throughout the day, especially in the resorts. Some continue to serve until after midnight.

**Shops.** In summer, spring and autumn, the siesta is still observed by many shops. Most are open Monday–Saturday 8am–1pm and 4–7pm (closing half an hour earlier or later depending upon season). There is no afternoon reopening on Wednesday and Saturday year-round. From October to April, there is no siesta; closing time is around 6pm.

## P

## PHOTOGRAPHY

For security reasons, you are not allowed to photograph military installations – especially along the border of the Turkish-controlled zone. In Northern Cyprus, be especially aware of this, as there are even more restricted areas there.

Taking photographs inside museums and churches with ancient icons is usually prohibited, although you may be permitted to take pictures without a flash. Don't be tempted to sneak a picture in places like Kykkos Monastery, as you may find yourself unceremoniously frogmarched to the door; and remember that flash photography damages the valuable medieval murals in some churches. As a matter of courtesy, always ask permission before attempting to photograph people, particularly monks and older people.

| May I take a picture? | **Boró na páro mía fotografía?** |

## POLICE

You probably won't see many policemen, but they are around and they invariably prove to be friendly and helpful if you need them. You'll recognise the traffic policemen by their white gloves and sleeves. Regular police officers in Southern Cyprus wear blue uniforms and they cruise around in blue-and-white police cars. Most members of the police speak some English.

**Police emergency numbers:**

In the South        112
In the North        155

| | |
|---|---|
| Where's the nearest police station? | **Pou íne to kondinótero astinomikó tmíma?** |

## POST OFFICES

District Post Offices, of which there are two in both Nicosia and Limassol, and one in both Larnaka and Pafos, are open Mon– Fri 7.30am–1.30pm and 3–6pm (4–7pm in July and Aug; closed Wednesday afternoons all year) and Sat 8.30–10.30am. All other post offices are open Mon–Fri 7.30am–1.30pm, plus Thur 3–6pm (closed Thursday afternoons in July and Aug).

**Postage stamps** may be bought at hotels, newsstands and kiosks. Postcards to Europe arrive within a week.

| | |
|---|---|
| Where's the (nearest) post office/telephone office? | **Pou íne to kodinótero tachidromío/cyta?** |
| A stamp for this letter/ postcard, please. | **Éna grammató simo giaftó to grámma/graftí tin kárta, parakaló.** |
| express/registered | **exprés/sistiméno** |
| airmail | **aeroporikós** |

## PUBLIC TRANSPORT

Cyprus has no railways and the inter-urban bus service is not always frequent, especially on Sundays. Bus services in the towns and resorts, however, are good, but service to and from villages – if it exists at all – is just one or two buses per day. Private and shared taxis fill the public transport gap.

**Private taxis.** Vehicles are metered and rates are relatively low, making private taxis a favourite form of transport in the South. Some visitors travel around the island exclusively by taxi *(see Guides and Tours on page113).* You can hail a taxi on the street or call for one by telephone. The numbers of the various private companies are listed in the local telephone directory.

**Shared service taxis and minibuses.** In the South, service taxis take from four to eight passengers and connect all major towns every half-hour. Ask the tourist office for a schedule *(see page 127).* Prices are fixed and very reasonable, so this is a good way to get from one town to another on a budget. In the North, minibuses called *dolmuş* operate between the towns but only depart when they are full.

| | |
|---|---|
| Where can I get a taxi/ shared taxi/ minibus? | **Pou boró na vro éna taxí/ epivatikó taxí/ mikro poúlman?** |
| May I have a place in this taxi for…? | **Thélo mía thési sto taxí giá…?** |
| What's the fare to…? | **Piá íne i timí giá…?** |

## R

## RELIGION

The native population of Southern Cyprus is almost 100 percent Greek Orthodox. The few mosques that you can still see are a reminder of the days before partition in 1974. Some are still used by Turkish Cypriots and Muslim residents and guest workers, however. There are several small Maronite Christian and Armenian Orthodox communities, and much larger numbers of Catholic and Protestant foreign residents and guest workers.

The Turkish Cypriot north of the island is primarily Muslim, but with Greek Orthodox, Maronite and other minorities.

It is important that you dress modestly when visiting churches, monasteries and mosques. The dress code for monasteries is usually rigidly enforced and specifies long trousers for men, a calf-length or longer skirt for women and covered shoulders for both sexes. Churches are generally less formal. You must remove your shoes before entering a mosque.

## T

## TELEPHONE

To call Southern Cyprus from abroad, the international dialling code is 357; for the North it is 90392. To call the UK from Cyprus, dial 00 for an international connection, then the country code 44 plus the area code (minus the initial 0), then the number. For the US, dial 001, then the area code, then the number. Other country codes are Australia: 61; Canada: 1; Ireland 353; New Zealand 64; South Africa: 27. For directory enquiries in Cyprus dial 192.

Public telephones can be used for local and international calls. All have instructions in English. A phone card, available in a selection of prices, is the simplest way to make an international call.

In most hotels, you can dial long-distance from your room, but the charges are high. Standard rates and other information are available from long-distance operators, all of whom speak English (tel: 194).

Area codes do not exist in Cyprus. Instead, there are eight-digit numbers in the South. In Nicosia, they start with 22; Agia Napa 23; Larnaka 24; Limassol 25; Pafos 26. In the North, numbers consist of seven digits, and localities can be determined by the first three.

## TIME DIFFERENCES

The chart on the next page shows the time differences between Cyprus, which is on Eastern European Time (EET), and various cities in winter (UTC/GMT + 2 hours). In summer, clocks are put forward 1 hour, so the time difference with the UK and US stays the same.

| New York | London | **Cyprus** | Jo'burg | Sydney | Auckland |
|----------|--------|------------|---------|--------|----------|
| 5am | 10am | **noon** | noon | 9pm | 11pm |

## TIPPING

Service charges are included in hotel, restaurant and taverna bills, but a little extra is always appreciated, especially for good service.

**Average tips:**

| | |
|---|---|
| Hotel porter, per bag | €2 |
| Maid, per day | €2 |
| Waiter/barman | 15 percent |
| Taxi driver | 10 percent |
| Tour guide (private) | around 10 percent |
| Tour guide (group tour) | from €2 per day |
| Hair stylist/barber | 10 percent |

## TOILETS

Public toilets exist in larger towns, but not in great numbers. Museums often have the cleanest facilities, and the ones on the government-run 'tourist beaches' are excellent. Generally standards are reasonable.

Toilets are usually indicated in both English and Greek. If you use the facilities in a café or restaurant, it is customary to buy something.

Where are the toilets?    **Pou íne ta apohoritíra?**

## TOURIST INFORMATION

The Cyprus Tourism Organisation, or CTO *(Kypriakós Organismós Tourismoú – KOT)*, which covers the South, is a mine of information, with free brochures and maps. The staff are knowledgeable and helpful.

**UK**          17 Hanover Street, London, W1S 1YP;
                tel: (020) 7569 8800; fax: (020) 7499 4935;
                email: <informationcto@btconnect.com>;
                <www.visitcyprus.org.cy>

**USA**         13 E 40th Street, New York, NY 10016;
                tel: (212) 683 5280; fax: (212) 683 5282;
                email: <gocyprus@aol.com>;
                <www.visitcyprus.com>

For information on Northern Cyprus:

**UK**          29 Bedford Square, London, WC1B 3EG;
                tel: (020) 7631 1930; fax: (020) 7462 9789;
                email: <info@go-northcyprus.com>;
                <www.tourism.trnc.net>

**USA**         1667 K Street, Suite 690, Washington DC, 20006;
                tel: (202) 887 6198; fax: (202) 467 0685;
                email: <kktc@erols.com>;
                <www.tourism.trnc.net>

The CTO's head office in Nicosia (not open to the public) is at 19 Leoforos Lemesou, PO Box 24535, 1390 Lefkosia; tel: 2269 1100; fax: 2233 1644; email: <cytour@cto.org.cy>; <www.visitcyprus. org.cy>. The CTO maintains offices at **Larnaka airport** (tel: 2464 3576); at **Pafos Airport** (tel: 2642 3161); at **Limassol harbour** (to meet ferries and cruise ships; tel: 2557 1868); and in the major tourist centres:

**Nicosia**     11 Odos Aristokyprou, Laïki Geitonia;
                tel: 2267 4264.
**Limassol**    115a Odos Spyrou Araouzou; tel: 2536 2756;
                22 Odos Georgiou A', Potamos tis Germasogeias;
                tel: 2532 3211.
**Larnaka**     Plateia Vasileos Pavlou; tel: 2465 4322.

| | |
|---|---|
| **Pafos** | 3 Odos Gladstonos, Ktima; tel: 2693 2841. |
| | 63a Leoforos Poseidonos, Kato Pafos; |
| | tel: 2693 0521. |
| **Agia Napa** | 12 Leoforos Kryou Nerou; tel: 2372 1796. |
| **Polis** | 2 Odos Vasileos Stasioikou A'; tel: 2632 2468. |
| **Pano Platres** | Plateia; tel: 2542 1316. (For the Troodos area visit the Pano Platres office.) |
| **Paralimni** | 356 Leoforos Protara-Kavo Gkreko, Paralimni; |
| **Protaras** | tel: 2383 2865. |

In Northern Cyprus, tourist information is available from the Ministry of Tourism, Lefkoşa, Turkish Republic of Northern Cyprus, c/o Mersin-10, Turkey; tel: 228 9629; fax: 227 3976; email: <info@holidayinnorthcyprus.com>; <www.holidayinnorth-cyprus.com>.

In addition, there are tourist offices in Keryneia/Girne (Kordon Boyu – the harbour; tel: 815 2145); Famagusta/Gazimağusa (Fevzi Çakmak Bulvarı; tel: 366 2864); and Nicosia/Lefkofla (at the Keryneia/Girne Gate; tel: 228 9629).

| | |
|---|---|
| Where's the tourist office? | **Pou íne to grafío tourismoú?** |

## W

## WATER

The island's tap water is peerfectly safe to drink, and still and sparkling mineral waters are bottled in Cyprus; imported bottled waters are widely available too.

| | |
|---|---|
| a bottle of mineral water | **éna boukáli metallikó neró** |
| fizzy (carbonated)/still | **me/chorís anthrakikó** |

## WEBSITES

The official website of the Cyprus Tourism Organisation is <www.visitcyprus.org.cy> (or <www.visitcyprus.com> or <www.cyprus tourism.org>). It's quite an entertaining site and provides basic information on several aspects of the island, but does not cover anything in great detail.

For information on Northern Cyprus visit <www.tourism.trnc.nct> and <www.holidayinnorthcyprus.com>.

Another website worth checking out before you set off for Cyprus is <www.windowoncyprus.com>, which carries mostly advertisements for local businesses (such as babysitting services and sports equipment hire shops), but also provides information about special events in various popular locations.

## WEIGHTS AND MEASURES

Cyprus uses the metric system. In the North, you may come across the old Ottoman system. There is an interesting anomaly in Southern Cyprus: beer is still often advertised by the pint (but the measure that you are served is half a litre).

## Y

## YOUTH HOSTELS

Only members of the Hostelling International Association may stay at Cyprus' youth hostels, and there are only two:

**Nicosia**    5 Odos Tefkrou; tel: 2267 4808.
**Larnaka**    27 Odos Nikolaou Rossou (near Agios Lazaros); tel: 2462 1188.

For further information about staying in youth hostels, contact the Cyprus Youth Hostels Association, PO Box 24040, 1700 Lefkosia, Cyprus; tel: 2267 0027; fax: 2267 2896.

## Recommended Hotels

With the exception of a new trend towards boutique hotels and spa resorts at the top end of the market, many beachfront hotels in Cyprus are much alike. All achieve an acceptable standard, but the rooms are often bland. All beach hotels offer watersports, while air-conditioning is standard in all but the most basic. All four- and five-star hotels have at least one restaurant, one pool and one tennis court, plus 24-hour room service. Their rooms all have satellite tv and a mini-bar.

Be aware that many hotels in Cyprus – both South and North – are block-booked by big tour operators so you should make reservations as early as possible. The Cyprus Hotel Association desk at Larnaka Airport can assist, as can the cto (see page 127). The symbols below a guide to prices (high season, double room, including breakfast).

| | |
|---|---|
| €€€€€ | over €240 (C£140) |
| €€€€ | €180–240 (C£105-C£140) |
| €€€ | €120–180 (C£70-C£105) |
| €€ | €60–120 (C£35-C£70) |
| € | under €60 (C£35) |

## SOUTHERN CYPRUS

## NICOSIA

**Averof €€** *19 Odos Averof; tel: 2277 3447; fax: 2277 3411; <www. averof.com.cy>*. This friendly, family-run two-star hotel is one of the best budget choices in town, a 15-minute walk from the old town walls and a 10-minute walk from the municipal pool. 25 rooms.

**Classic €€** *94 Odos Rigainis; tel: 2266 4006; fax: 2236 0072; <www.classic.com.cy>*. This hotel lies just within the city walls near Pafos Gate, a 10-minute walk from the Ledra Palace Hotel checkpoint. It has small but comfortable bedrooms, a lively cocktail bar, an excellent restaurant (Fifty-Nine Knives, *see page 137*) and a small but well-equipped gym, all of which belie its two-star rating. 57 rooms.

**Cyprus Hilton €€€€€** *Leoforos Archiepiskopou Makariou III; tel: 2237 7777; fax: 2237 7788; <www.hilton.com>.* This five-star hotel is in a relatively quiet setting back from the main road, a 15-minute drive from the old town. It has three restaurants and excellent sports facilities, including a pool, tennis courts and health club. 298 rooms.

**Holiday Inn Nicosia €€€** *70 Odos Rigainis; tel: 2271 2712; fax: 2267 3337; <www.ichotelsgroup.com>.* This four-star hotel features its own Japanese restaurant *(see page 137)*, swimming pool and health club, and has a good location just within the city walls close to Plateia Eleftherias. 140 rooms.

## LARNAKA

**Flamingo Beach €€** *152 Leoforos Piyale Paşa; tel: 2482 8224; fax: 2465 6564; <www.flamingobeachhotel.com>.* This family-run, three-star seafront hotel lies on the southern edge of town, just after the fort, at the start of Mackenzie Beach. All rooms have a seaview balcony. Rooftop pool. 64 rooms.

**Golden Bay €€€€€** *Larnaka–Dekeleia road; tel: 2464 5444; fax: 2464 5451; <www.goldenbay.com.cy>.* This five-star beach-front hotel lies 8km (5 miles) east of town and is set in land-scaped water gardens. Rooms and suites are of a high standard. Excellent leisure and health facilities include an outdoor Jacuzzi. 193 rooms.

**Sandy Beach €€** *Larnaka–Dekeleia road; tel: 2464 6333; fax: 2464 6900; <www.sandybeachhotel.com.cy>.* Friendly four-star beachfront hotel on Larnaka Bay, 7km (4 miles) east of town, with tavernas, bars and restaurants within walking distance. Indoor and outdoor swimming pools, good health club and gym. 205 rooms.

**Sun Hall €€** *6 Leoforos Athinou; tel: 2465 3341; fax: 2465 2717; <www.aquasolhotels.com>.* A four-star hotel right in the centre of the action on the main Palm Tree Promenade, opposite the beach and marina. Health club and gym, but no swimming pool. 114 rooms.

## AGIA NAPA AND REGION

**Asterias Beach €€** *Makronisos, Agia Napa; tel: 2372 1901; fax: 2372 2095; email: <asterias.beach.hotel@cytanet.com.cy>.* Set on the edge of town on the popular sandy beach of Makronisos, this well-equipped four-star hotel has its own swimming pool and tennis courts, and many other facilities. 198 rooms.

**Grecian Park €€€€** *81 Odos Konnos, Konnos Bay, Protaras; tel: 2384 4000; fax: 2384 4001; <www.grecianpark.com>.* Set halfway between Agia Napa and Protaras, this five-star hotel enjoys a fine hilltop location overlooking sandy Konnos Bay beach. It features luxurious public areas, a large free-form swimming pool and a grassy sunbathing terrace with great sea views. 240 rooms.

**Louis Nausicaa Beach €€** *17 Odos Syttarkas, Protaras; tel: 2383 1160; fax: 2383 1519; <www.louishotel.com>.* These classy low-rise apartments enjoy a great location on a promontory overlooking beautiful Fig Tree Bay and the island's best sandy beaches. Accommodation is spacious, comfortable and stylish, with a whitewashed Mediterranean theme. 205 rooms.

## LIMASSOL (LEMESOS)

**Ajax €€** *Corner of Odos Damon and Odos D. Nikolaou, Mesa Geitonia; tel: 2559 0000; fax: 2559 1222; <www.ajaxhotel.com>.* This recently renovated modern four-star hotel is set between the tourist area of Potamos Germasogeias and the town centre, about 1km (½ mile) from the beach. Facilities include outdoor and indoor pools, floodlit tennis courts, a health club and a kids' club. 176 rooms.

**Amathus Beach €€€€€** *Amathous; tel: 2583 2000; fax: 2583 2540; <www.amathushotel.com>.* This five-star beachfront hotel set 9km (6 miles) east of the city centre has extensive landscaped grounds, a spa and wellness centre, and two swimming pools, one of which has underwater music. In summer, the hotel runs its own beachside fish taverna. 239 rooms.

## TROODOS MOUNTAINS

**Churchill Pinewood Valley €€** *Pedoulas; tel: 2295 2211; fax: 2295 2439; email: <pinewood@churchill.com.cy>.* Between Pedoulas and Prodromos, this three-star mountain-lodge-style hotel is set in its own lovely, secluded cherry orchard and pine forest, with landscaped gardens and a tea terrace. Rooms are comfortable and tastefully decorated. Swimming pool, tennis court, gym, sauna and children's playground. 49 rooms.

**Forest Park Hotel €€** *Pano Platres; tel: 2542 1751; fax: 2542 1875; <www.forestparkhotel.com.cy>.* Nestling in its own forest, the four-star Forest Park offers many of the creature comforts of its beachside counterparts, including a heated outdoor pool and an indoor pool. It is within walking distance of Pano Platres village. 137 rooms.

**Linos Inn €€** *34 Odos Palaias, Kakopetria; tel: 2292 3161; fax: 2292 3181; <www.linos-inn.com.cy>.* This beautifully restored group of old village houses offers a romantic and homely setting with lots of antique fittings and furnishings. Facilities include mini-bars and satellite TV, sauna and Jacuzzi, and an attractive traditional restaurant. 22 rooms.

## PAFOS AND REGION

**Alexander the Great €€€** *Leoforos Poseidonos, Pafos; tel: 2696 5000; fax: 2696 5100; <www.kanikahotels.com>.* Located on the best stretch of town beach, this four-star hotel is close to all town centre activities. Sporting facilities include outdoor and indoor pools and tennis courts. Health and beauty club. 202 rooms.

**Annabelle €€€€€** *Leoforos Poseidonos, Pafos; tel: 2693 8333; fax: 2694 5502; <www.theannabellehotel.com>.* This refined, luxury five-star beachfront hotel is in the centre of town overlooking the harbour. Attractive gardens surround the pool. Rooms are large and well-furnished. Good sports facilities and restaurant. 198 rooms.

**Cynthiana Beach €€** *Kisonerga; tel: 2693 3900; fax: 2694 4648; <www.cynthianahotel.com>.* This three-star beachfront hotel is about 8km (5 miles) west of town on a headland, in large land-scaped gardens flanked by banana plantations, with a sandy beach immediately below. Indoor and outdoor swimming pools, tennis courts and other sports facilities. 230 rooms.

**Kiniras €€** *91 Leoforos Archiepiskopou Makariou III; tel: 2694 1604; fax: 2694 2176; <www.kiniras.cy.net>.* If you don't need a beachfront setting or four-star luxury, this charming small hotel is a traditional 70-year-old house with public areas beautifully decorated in rustic style. Rooms are plain but comfortable. Although it's on the upper town's main street, it is quiet at night. No pool but the municipal baths are just 200m (220yds) away. 18 rooms.

**Leptos Coral Beach €€€€€** *Coral Beach; tel: 2688 1000; fax: 2662 2930; <www.coral.com.cy>.* Some 12km (7 miles) north of Pafos, this highly rated luxury five-star resort is a perfect place to escape the bustle of town, with lush landscaped gardens that open directly onto a sandy beach. There is an extensive range of leisure facilities, including a health and beauty spa, floodlit tennis courts, an archery range and an innovative arts and crafts centre, where guests can learn glass painting, pottery and ceramic painting. 421 rooms.

**Riu Cypria Maris Beach €€€** *Leoforos Poseidonos, Geroskipou; tel: 2696 4111; fax: 2696 4125; <www.riu.com>.* This smart four-star hotel 3km (2 miles) east of the harbour features a little more style and character than other comparable Pafos accommodation. Extensive palm-shaded gardens surround the pool and lead directly onto the beach. 40 rooms.

**Roman €€** *Odos Agiou Lamprianou; tel: 2694 5411; fax 2694 6834; <www.romanhotel.com.cy>*. Perfectly positioned, just 1km (½ mile) from the town centre and a five-minute walk from the beach, the three-star Roman has the look of an ancient monument from the outside, while the interior is a daring and fanciful exercise in ancient Roman-style décor with bold wall paintings, colourful mosaics and other 'Roman' paraphernalia. Small swimming pool. 87 rooms.

## NORTHERN CYPRUS

## NORTHERN NICOSIA (LEFKOŞA)

**Saray €€€** *Atatürk Meydani; tel: 228 3115; fax: 228 4408; email: <saray@northcyprus.net>*. Dating from the 1950s – and looking it, despite refurbishment – this is nevertheless the top hotel in the Turkish-Cypriot part of the capital. It offsets its somewhat undistinguished character with reasonable comfort, a fine position on the northern sector's main square, and a rooftop bar and restaurant with a great view over the city. 72 rooms.

## KERYNEIA (GIRNE)

**Dome €€€** *Kordonboyu; tel: 815 2453; fax: 815 2772; <www.domehotelcyprus.com>*. This stylish waterfront hotel near the harbour still retains some of its colonial-heyday cachet, despite the casino that has been added to boost revenues. Its cosmopolitan air is complemented by well-equipped rooms, many of them with views, and a fair restaurant that serves both Turkish and international cuisine. 160 rooms.

## FAMAGUSTA (GAZIMAĞUSA)

**Bilfer Palm Beach €€€€** *Deve Limani; tel: 366 2000; fax: 366 2002; <www.bilferhotel.com>*. Pastel-toned and graceful, the hotel stands right up against Famagusta's abandoned and derelict former Greek Cypriot suburb, Varosha. The Palm Beach resolutely averts its eyes, focusing instead on its own chic interior and de luxe lifestyle, and on the superb beach located out front. 108 rooms.

## Recommended Restaurants

During the summer season, restaurants that are open all day generally operate from 9.30am–11pm. Those that only serve lunch and dinner are usually open 12–3pm and 6.30–11.30pm. If you are planning a special journey to a restaurant in low season, it's always advisable to call ahead to confirm opening hours, as some places close early or open late out of season.

Average meal prices, which are controlled by the government, are remarkably uniform (though fish dishes are more expensive), so don't be surprised to find that most places listed below fall into the moderate price bracket. Prices relate to a three-course meal (or a meze) per person, excluding drinks.

€€€    over €40 (C£23)
€€     €15–40 (C£9–C£23)
€      under €15 (C£9)

## SOUTHERN CYPRUS

## NICOSIA

**Abu Faysal €€** *31 Odos Klimentos; tel: 2276 0353.* Open daily for lunch and dinner. Excellent Lebanese food is served in a relaxing atmosphere, especially so in warm weather when the garden (which also serves as an art gallery) is open. Jazz musicians perform on occasional evenings in winter.

**Arhondiko €€** *27 Odos Aristokyprou, Laïki Geitonia; tel: 2268 0080.* Open all day Monday to Saturday, and from 5pm on Sunday. This pretty little restaurant occupies a romantic setting with tables under the trees, in the heart of the restored, pedestrian Laïki Geitonia district. Try the traditional *meze*, stuffed vegetables, quail or pilaf, or push the boat out with gilthead sea bream.

**Bonzai €€€** *Holiday Inn Nicosia, 70 Odos Rigainis; tel: 2271 2712.* Open daily for lunch and dinner. You can partake of

Nicosia's more cosmopolitan character, when compared with the resorts, and take a break from Cypriot cuisine at this tolerably fine, if not quite rigorous Japanese restaurant. *Teppan yaki* and *sushi* dishes are served in a relaxed and friendly ambience.

**Fifty-Nine Knives €€–€€€** *Classic Hotel, 94 Odos Rigainis; tel: 2266 4006.* Open daily for lunch and dinner (closed for dinner August). The name refers to an archaeological find below the present building, and this excellent little restaurant is a discovery in itself. Ultramodern and stylish without being intimidating, it serves innovative Cypriot dishes with an international twist, as well as some interesting international dishes at reasonable prices.

**Matheos €** *Plateia 28 Oktovriou; tel: 2275 5846.* Open daily all day. A no-frills locals' place, Matheos is recommended by everyone and is used to tourists. They serve all the usual favourites, but try something seasonal, such as quail or rabbit with pilaf. It's easy to find (at the back of the Faneromeni Church, beside the tiny mosque) and has outdoor and indoor seating.

## LARNAKA

**1900 Art Café €€** *6 Odos Stasinou; tel: 2465 3027.* Open daily 6pm–midnight. Charming and arty, this café-restaurant is set in a lovely early 20th-century house opposite the Pierides Museum. Downstairs, among the artworks, drinks and snacks are served, while upstairs is an excellent, inventive restaurant. Home-cooked dishes include chicken in honey and lemon; chicken with orange juice, thyme and garlic; *távas* (traditional lamb or pork stew); stuffed vegetables and other vegetarian options. The café is run by a local radio celebrity and often on Friday evenings there is live music.

**I Mavri Chelona €€** *11 Odos Mehmet Ali; tel: 2465 0661.* Open daily noon–midnight. Larnaka's old Turkish Quarter is home to some of the town's oldest and best restaurants, a description that does justice to 'The Black Turtle'. The upstairs dining room has old-fashioned charm to go along with smooth service and a menu that takes in some traditional home-cooking dishes.

**Militzis €€** *42 Odos Piyale Paşa; tel: 2465 5867.* Open daily noon–midnight. Just south of the fort, Militzis has a windmill on its front terrace. A short meat-only menu features no-nonsense dishes such as *kokoretsi* (offal), *zalatina* (brawn/jellied pork), *kefalaki* (lamb's head) and more conventional grills and casseroles. *Kléftiko* (oven-roasted lamb) is a house speciality. Takeaway is available.

**Varoshiotis Seafood Restaurant €€** *7 Odos Piyale Paşa, corner of Odos Sakarya; tel: 7777 7708.* Open daily for lunch and dinner. One of the best fish tavernas in town, it has been catering for locals as well as visitors since 1964. Try the fish *meze* – or just ask for whatever is fresh off the fishing boats that day.

## AGIA NAPA AND REGION

**Esperia €€** *46 Leoforos Archiepiskopou Makariou III, Agia Napa; tel: 2372 1635.* Open May–Oct daily 8am–midnight; Nov–Apr Mon–Fri 8am–5pm, Sat–Sun 8am–7pm. Right on the harbour, seafood is the main fare here (although the menu also has meat dishes). Ask for whatever is fresh off the fishing boats moored beside your table, rather than be served with something imported and frozen. Accompanied by a village salad, a light Cypriot wine – and that harbour view – your meal should be memorable.

**Limelight Taverna €€** *Odos Lipertis (opposite the post office), Agia Napa; tel: 2372 1650.* Open daily all day. A long-standing and reliable performer in the resort, this is the best grill house in town for steaks, but is also recommended for lamb, suckling pig and *souvláki*, all cooked over charcoal.

**Potamos €€** *Limanaki, Potamos tou Liopetri; tel: 9965 8243.* Open summer Tues–Sun 10am–11pm; winter Tues–Sun 10am–9pm. Taste is the unique selling point of this indelibly Cypriot seafood taverna, which is right beside the fishing boats at Potamos Creek. Few indeed are the concessions made either to sensitive foreign palates or twee restaurant design expectations. The food is authentic enough to be eaten by the fishermen who have just brought it ashore and the service is unornamented.

**To Ploumin €€** *3 Odos Oktovriou 28, Sotira; tel: 9965 8333.* Usually open daily for lunch and dinner, but check in advance. This charming traditional taverna of formica-topped tables and Van Gogh-style wicker chairs was built in 1938 and is now a listed building. With displays of old tools, pottery, furniture and handicrafts, it is perfect for a home-cooked *meze*.

## LIMASSOL (LEMESOS)

**Karatello €€–€€€** *Odos Vasilissis; tel: 2582 0464.* Open daily for dinner. A renovated carob mill and warehouse from around 1900 close to the castle is the setting for this ultramodern and chic restaurant – an indicator of the direction in which the Cypriot dining scene is moving. The kitchen takes Cypriot and Greek stalwarts and serves them in updated form, with elements of fusion and other experimental styles.

**The Old Harbour–Ladas Fish Tavern €€–€€€** *Old Harbour; tel: 2536 5760.* Open Monday to Saturday for lunch and dinner. An atmospheric and friendly place at the old port that has been going strong for 50 years, and claims to be the oldest fresh fish taverna in Limassol. It is certainly one of the best, with an excellent selection of the best quality fish straight off the adjacent boats, usually simply grilled over charcoal. Popular with locals and visitors.

## TROODOS MOUNTAINS

**Linos Inn €€–€€€** *Old Kakopetria; tel: 2292 3161.* Open daily for lunch and dinner. A splendidly renovated taverna in an Alpine-looking setting of beautifully restored village houses *(see page 133)* in Old Kakopetria. Excellent, carefully prepared and inventive regional and Cypriot dishes.

**The Mill €€–€€€** *8 Odos Mylou, Old Kakopetria; tel: 2292 2536.* Open daily for lunch and dinner. Set on the top floor of a hotel in a beautifully converted mill, this rambling and veteran restaurant is an experience in itself. Book a table on the small outside balcony if possible. The local speciality, fresh (farmed) trout, is almost *de rigueur* here, but the *souvláki* and *kléftiko* are also good.

**Psilo Dhendhro €€** *Platres–Limassol road; tel: 2542 1350.* Open daily 11am–5pm. A trout farm on the premises ensures that your choice of meal is just about decided for you at this popular and attactive establishment. A perfect place for rest and refreshment after walking the scenic trail to the Kalidonia waterfall *(see page 59)*, which starts and finishes here. Book before you set off.

## PAFOS AND REGION

**Cavallini €€€** *Leoforos Poseidonos (next to Amathus hotel), Kato Pafos; tel: 2696 4164.* Open Monday to Saturday from 7pm. Probably the best Italian restaurant in town, Cavallini offers sophisticated dining from a wide-ranging northern Italian menu, served in a stylish but cosy interior and on a lovely terrace that's unfortunately subjected to traffic noise.

**Chez Alex €€€** *7 Odos Konstantia (corner of Odos Tefkrou), Kato Pafos; tel: 2693 4767.* Open daily for lunch and dinner. In a quiet part of the central nightlife area, this is among the town's best fish restaurants. If it swims, they cook it – give three hours' notice for their specials of Surprise Sea Bream (baked in a salt crust) or *bouillabaisse*; 12 hours' notice for lobster. Dining room with terrace.

**Demokritos €€** *1 Odos Dionysou, Kato Pafos; tel: 2693 3371.* Open nightly. It's hard to miss Demokritos – just follow the crowds, who later sit wide-eyed at the glass-balancing acts of its staff. Open since 1971, it is the oldest taverna-restaurant in Pafos. It trades more heavily on its music and dancing than its food, which is inevitably compromised due to numbers. But it's still a good night out.

**Kiniras €€** *91 Leoforos Archiepiskopou Makariou III, Ktima (Upper Pafos); tel: 2694 1604.* Open daily for lunch and dinner, or for drinks at any time. The garden courtyard of the Kiniras hotel *(see page 134)* is one of the nicest places to eat on the island. The food is excellent and portions are hearty. The menu features some inventive international dishes, but ask the charming proprietor, George, for his recommendation and you will probably be steered towards a traditional favourite such as *kléftiko* or *stifado*. Highly recommended.

**Paphos Grill House €** *Corner of Odos Iakovidhi and Odos Ioannis Agrotis, Ktima (Upper Pafos); tel: 2693 8031.* Open Monday to Saturday all day. After visiting the nearby museums, it's nice to take a seat under a parasol, either on the street corner, or on the edge of the adjacent gardens. Don't look for anything fancy here. Simple grills are the hallmark of this basic, owner-managed locals' restaurant. Service can be slow.

**Pelican €€** *The Harbour, Kato Pafos; tel: 2694 6886.* Open daily all day. Occupying a smart terrace on the harbourfront, the Pelican is probably the best of several unspectacular tavernas that compete for customers here, in a setting that's so scenic that tables are always in demand. Go for a fish *meze* or a swordfish special.

**Peyia Tavern €€** *Leoforos Kyprianou, Pegeia; tel: 2662 1077.* Open daily for dinner. A burgeoning village north of Pafos, just inland from Coral Bay, has long had a cluster of fine traditional tavernas on and around its main square. This one serves no-frills home cooking in a plain old-fashioned setting, or on a tiny terrace out front, and fills up quickly every evening.

**Seacrest €€–€€€** *Lakki Harbour; tel: 2632 1333.* Open daily all day. You probably won't go wrong at any of Lakki's harbourside restaurants, as they all serve fish straight from the boat to the oven. Seacrest is one of the best, with a perfect harbour view. Splurge on the Seacrest Special – lobster stuffed with sole and crabmeat.

**Seven St George's Tavern €€** *Odos Pavlou Krinaiou, Geroskipou, just off the main road to Kato Pafos; tel: 2696 3176.* Open Tuesday to Sunday for lunch and dinner. It's not easy to find this charming garden taverna, but it is well worth the effort. George and Lara, the affable owners, offer what could well be the best *meze* on the island (including a vegetarian option). The quality of the food, the range of dishes, the service and the atmosphere are light years away from the anonymous *moussaka*-and-chips joints of Kato Pafos.

**Ta Bagnia €€** *Leoforos Poseidonos, Kato Pafos; tel: 2694 1558*. Open daily all day. Set right on the seafront in a busy part of town, Ta Bagnia means 'the baths', referring to the municipal swimming pool immediately next door. It's a popular, friendly and enjoyable place to catch the breeze, and is surprisingly sheltered from the hubbub. The atmosphere is that of a bright, blue-and-white Mediterranean seaside café. A wide range of snacks and full meals is on offer, though the quality of the latter is variable.

## NORTHERN CYPRUS

## NORTHERN NICOSIA (LEFKOŞA)

**Saray Roof €€€** *In the Saray Hotel, Atatürk Meydanı; tel: 228 3115*. It would be more accurate to say 'on the Saray Hotel'. A superb rooftop location with an unbeatable view over the city is this restaurant's unique selling point. The Turkish and Continental dishes on the menu are polished enough, but don't quite reach the heights.

## KERYNEIA (GIRNE)

**Canlı Balık €€** *Kordonboyou; tel: 815 2182*. Open daily for lunch and dinner. Probably the best of the many fish restaurants in at the splendid Keryneia harbour, Canlı Balik enjoys an elevated centre-stage view of one of the island's most scenic settings and serves consistently good fish dishes. Ideal for lunch.

## FAMAGUSTA (GAZIMAĞUSA)

**La Veranda €** *Nemık Kemal Meydanı; tel: 367 0153*. Plain, wholesome Turkish fare that doesn't extend much beyond kebabs and salads – but good ones – keeps the customers satisfied on the outdoor terrace in the city's main square, with a romantic view of the Lala Mustafa Paşa Mosque and the Venetian governor's palace.

# INDEX

**Berlitz** pocket guide

# Cyprus

**Seventh Edition 2008**

**Written by** Paul Murphy
**Updated by** George McDonald
**Principal photographer:** Caroline Jones
**Edited by** Alex Knights
**Series Editor:** Tony Halliday

Printed in Singapore by Insight Print
Services (Pte) Ltd, 38 Joo Koon Road,
Singapore 628990. Tel: (65) 6865-1600.
Fax: (65) 6861-6438

Berlitz Trademark Reg. U.S. Patent Office
and other countries. Marca Registrada

Photography credits
Caroline Jones 7, 10, 13, 14, 17, 18, 24, 26, 28, 29,
32, 36, 39, 40, 46, 48, 49, 51, 53, 54, 55, 56, 57, 59,
60, 64, 67, 68, 69, 72, 73, 80, 82, 84, 86, 92, 95; Jon
Davison 22, 31; Paul Murphy 6, 8, 15, 45, 50, 58,
65, 76, 89, 96, 100; George Taylor 20, 35, 37, 38,
42, 44, 62, 71, 75, 78, 79, 81, 90, 99

Cover picture: Robert Harding

Every effort has been made to provide
accurate information in this publication,
but changes are inevitable. The publisher
cannot be responsible for any resulting
loss, inconvenience or injury.

**Contact us**

At Berlitz we strive to keep our guides as
accurate and up to date as possible, but if you
find anything that has changed, or if you have
any suggestions on ways to improve this guide,
then we would be delighted to hear from you.

Berlitz Publishing, PO Box 7910,
London SE1 1WE, England
fax: (44) 20 7403 0290
email: berlitz@apaguide.co.uk
www.berlitzpublishing.com